PARTNERSHIP IN LAY SPIRITUALITY

Flu

Maureen Dolan

Partnership in
Lay Spirituality

RELIGIOUS AND LAITY FIND NEW WAYS

the columba press

First published in 2007 by
the columba press
55A Spruce Avenue, Stillorgan Industrial Park,
Blackrock, Co Dublin

Cover by Bill Bolger
Origination by The Columba Press
Printed in Ireland by ColourBooks Ltd, Dublin

ISBN 978 1 85607 563 3

Table of Contents

Foreword

The Second Vatican Council (1962-1965) ushered in a new springtime for the church, touching all aspects of its self-understanding, life and members. The council also made important contributions to theology and pastoral practice. The clerical church of the post-Tridentine period gave way to new developments for laity and religious. On the one hand, the council gave great encouragement to religious to renew themselves and their congregations, taking special account of their heritage, of their founding charism and of the needs of the contemporary world. On the other hand, laity were challenged by the universal call to holiness found in the council's central document, *The Constitution on the Church* (chap 5). At first religious and laity sought to answer this call in their own way, but soon there would be an exciting new development as religious and laity together found a new approach to fulfilling the vision of the council. There was a convergence of interests as laity sought a viable spirituality and religious tried to show their charism as relevant for the contemporary world.

This current phenomenon goes by various names, such as lay association, affiliation or lay associate membership of a religious institute; the reality is sharing in the charism, life and spirituality of religious institutes by lay people. One could point to a variety of reasons why the charism of religious institutes seems to attract lay people, so that they want their Christian lives to be formed and guided by a charism originally given to religious men and women in another age.

There is of course the contemporary interest in spirituality – an interest that is hard to evaluate. In this context we find spiritualities of religious purified from many off-putting accessories so that the beauty and drawing power of a founding charism emerges in a fresh and attractive way. Another reason for the success of new associations is that they offer an integral vision; over many years religious acquired a wisdom that led them to avoid distortions or harmful excesses in the spiritual life. The heritage of religious life has borne fruit in many great works for the church and society, as well as producing many outstanding examples of holiness. But, above all, this new interest in associations is a work of the Holy Spirit who continually draws new things from the old, and is now invigorating religious institutes and giving new possibilities to the dream of Vatican II of the universal call to holiness for laity, clergy and religious.

Maureen Dolan has written important book in an area where there is little accessible material. She presents the new phenomenon of lay association. Her book begins by outlining the history of lay spirituality. In the first millennium, and even up to the Reformation, she sees lay people as having existed on crumbs that fell from the spiritual tables of clergy and religious. But even then there were people and ideas that in time would be a powerful stimulus for lay life. She brings us through developments in theology, spirituality, in the teachings of councils, popes and spiritual leaders, as well as in canon law, right up to the end of the 20th century.

There are many kinds of association with religious. Maureen Dolan has had first-hand experience through being Director of the Lay Association of the Daughters of Mary and Joseph. This was originally a Belgian congregation, but in time it spread to the United Kingdom and Ireland, to the United States as well as Africa. She consulted widely with religious congregations of men and women so that she presents a coherent picture of this new experience in the church. She shows that though very significant in the contemporary church, association has much earlier roots in third orders and similar groupings. Her research and experience allows her to make important observations about the strengths and weaknesses found in lay associations. She shows too how there can be tensions and rich resources in having women and men associated with congregations that were originally for one sex only. She also gives guidance to both the religious and the laity involved in this new development in spirituality.

I recommend very highly this book to laity, religious and clergy. It will open up for many people fresh possibilities of the Christian vocation.

Christopher O'Donnell, O Carm
Milltown Institute of Theology and Philosophy,
Dublin 6.

Carmelite Institute
Rome.

Introduction

One of the greatest challenges facing the church is to fill the hunger within people's hearts for meaning and for a spirituality. There is within the church today, not so much a crisis of faith as a crisis in spirituality. Many people are not hostile to the church but find that the institutional church has little or no relevance for their daily lives.

In the years since the Second Vatican Council, forty years ago, many lay people have become aware of the radical call of all to holiness, and of their responsibility to share in the mission of the church through baptism and confirmation.

However, when many of these same people have sought to respond to that call of Vatican II, they have become disillusioned and frustrated. Instead of finding a church of sharing, participation (*communio*) and openness, they have in some instances found a hierarchical church which they perceived as cold or negative. They also found a church which was unable to offer them a spirituality fully satisfying for their lay state. This is the same church which has struggled in the last two thousand years to come to terms with the definition of who a lay person is.

Since most of my adult life has been lived in the Post-Vatican II period, I was aware, perhaps vaguely and not fully in an articulate fashion, of these problems surrounding lay spirituality. In the mid-1980s, I had the good fortune to be invited to be part of a new venture within the Congregation of the Daughters of Mary and Joseph (DMJ), namely, lay associate membership. My own experience has been of enrichment in spirituality. This led me to undertake further study in spirituality and theology in the Milltown Institute, Dublin.

The first part of this book deals with issues of lay spirituality. The first chapter seeks to understand what spirituality is, and goes on to develop the notion of a lay spirituality which is essential to the church and its mission.

The following chapter surveys the place of laity in New Testament times. It proceeds to look at the early centuries, some trends and heresies that had a negative influence on the role of laity in the church and spirituality. It traces the development of the laity through the Middle Ages to the beginning of the twentieth century, zooming in on developments that positively or negatively reflected on the place of the laity in the church. It will become apparent that there is a problem with the role and identity of the laity in the church which in turn gives rise to the need of having a spirituality that is suitable to the lay state.

The third chapter situates some twentieth-century movements in relationship to Vatican II insights. It looks at the Council's work on the laity and developments up to the revision of Canon Law (1983).

With chapter four we begin the second part of the book. We narrow the focus on lay spirituality to a recent phenomen of lay associate membership of a religious congregation. Church legislation from the early twentieth century prepared for this new reality which emerged strongly after the council.

In the fifth chapter we examine key elements of associate membership. These include (1) charism/gift of the Holy Spirit; (2) spirituality/prayer life; (3) community/family spirit/togetherness; (4) mission/ministry/apostolate/social concern; (5) commitment/response; (5) formation/growth. Finally the chapter investigates the need for some legislation and structures.

The concluding chapter considers the contribution of associate membership to lay spirituality and the church. This new development is one way in which religious and laity are responding to this challenge, seeing it as a 'sign of the times'. The chapter ends by evaluating some of the strengths and weaknesses of associate membership.

I am deeply indebted to many people who have made it possible for me to complete this book. I want particularly to say thanks to family members. I wish to express my gratitude to Father Christopher O'Donnell O Carm., of the Milltown Institute of Theology and Spirituality who directed the original research, for his guidance, wisdom, and encouragement, and for writing the Foreword. I thank my sister Bridie and Sr Máire O'Donnell RSHM for their careful reading and correcting of the manuscript. I would like to pay special tribute to the Daughters of Mary and Joseph who have shown so much interest in my work. In particular I would like to thank Sister Teresa Clements DMJ who made information for my research available to me.

I am grateful to all the DMJ Sisters who aided me in my research by completing questionnaires. I felt the support of DMJ Associates through their interest in my writing and in completing a long questionnaire.

I would like to express my special gratitude to all the provincials and superiors of religious congregations in Ireland who provided me with information regarding associate membership in their respective institutes.

I hope that people may find in lay associate membership a new vital aid in following Christ.

Maureen Dolan
Feast of All Saints 2006

CHAPTER ONE

Spirituality and the Laity

The years 2002 to 2005 marked the fortieth anniversary of Vatican II. When we look at the work of the council there are three main texts of great importance for lay life in the church. These are chapter four of the Constitution on the Church (*Lumen gentium, LG*), the Constitution on the Church in the Modern World (*Gaudium et spes, GS*) and the Decree on the Laity (*Apostolicam actuositatem, AA*). Commentaries and evaluations are still emerging. It would probably be hard to find many people generally satisfied with the church in the four decades since the council. Some will blame the council for a decline in church membership and vitality. Others will claim that the promise of the council has been a disappointment. They can speak darkly of inertia or a high-jacking of the council mandate by conservative forces.

One encounters such negative thinking frequently among laity on the subject of lay spirituality. There had been a promise of renewed participation and challenges. But apart from involvement in liturgy by a tiny minority of the laity, their state in many ways would seem not to have improved significantly since the council. This, of course, is to take the negative view but it does point to the fact that structural changes in law, organisation or even pastoral planning do not seem to hold out any immediate promise of radical improvement of the laity's position.

If it is true that structural changes have proved disappointing, perhaps it is time to focus on a more positive development arising from the universal call to holiness outlined in the radical fifth chapter of the Constitution on the Church. It is this call surely that should be the foundation of all renewal. Indeed, one can point to fresh interest in spirituality in our world today. One of the most important developments in the latter half of the twentieth century was a re-presentation of the nature of holiness

12

through saints like Thérèse of Lisieux. She had promoted a simple approach to God in a basic response to his outreaching love. Many people in the mid-twentieth century still perceived holiness as *doing* many things, especially extended prayer and penance. The few canonised saints who were lay lived lives that seemed remote from the situation or possibilities of most lay people.

However Vatican Two put down a clear marker stating:

It is therefore quite clear that all Christians in whatever state or walk in life are called to the fullness of the Christian life and the perfection of charity. (*LG* 40)

Holiness in Vatican II terms stressed a sharing in the divine nature, the acceptance of the gifts of the Holy Spirit, allowing ourselves to be conformed to the image of Christ. This document goes on to show the special call to holiness for bishops and clergy and for married couples, adding however, 'in a different way a similar example is given by widows, widowers and single people, who can greatly contribute to the holiness of the church' (*LG* 41). Religious are not specifically mentioned as chapter six addresses their particular calling.

In this book we will explore the notion of Christian spirituality, and its development through the ages. More specifically, we will consider lay spirituality in order to grasp and evaluate a new phenomenon in the church in which lay people are now sharing in the charism of a religious congregation through lay associate membership. This is a new reality which is a mutual enrichment of laity and religious that can be found when together they seek holiness according to a variety of charisms given to the church through religious families (see *LG* 43).

Holiness for Lay People

Lay people live out the implications of the Christian message largely in a secular environment. An authentic lay spirituality must speak to individual life situations, joys and sorrows, such as family celebrations, unemployment, sickness, job promotion, retirement. If we were to take five states – a parish priest, a married mother, a single active person, a single retired sick person and a contemplative religious – it would be clear that there will be a far greater difference in the way that they observe the second commandment of loving neighbour rather than the first commandment of loving God. The difference will be in the way love is expressed. Thus the great text in Micah will be lived differently by each of the above.

This is what Yahweh asks of you, only this:

That you act justly,

That you love tenderly,

That you walk humbly with your God. (Micah 6:8)

The Eucharist, source and climax of the spiritual life, will be where the lay person draws strength for secular involvement and it also gives ultimate meaning to that involvement.

There must be no blurring of the notion of the secular but one must avoid a false division that would suggest that the church is where the clergy's activities take place and the laity are involved only in matters of the world. Clergy and laity are both church. The clergy serve the laity who in turn act in the world. It will be clear that the balance and emphasis given to the various elements common to all spirituality will vary.

We have begun to use the word spirituality as if its meaning were self evident. We need to look in greater depth at the notion of spirituality itself before taking up the difficult and controverted issue of lay spirituality. If we visit a book store today we will almost certainly see a section on spirituality. Books about spirituality abound. We will discover books on New Age spirituality, transcendental meditation, ecology, feminist spirituality. In a religious book store there will be a myriad of books on spirituality ranging from books on the study of spirituality to Marian spirituality, to Christian spirituality, to Eastern spirituality, to lay spirituality to name but a few. However, when we attempt to define the word we immediate run into some confusion. Writers and authors define the word with limited success. Many dictionaries and encyclopaedias still do not have a major entry on spirituality and refer rather to 'spiritual experience', 'spiritual development' or some such. In its original English usage it applied to the clergy or church matters, as opposed to the secular; things of the spirit such as the soul, or a spirit as distinct from material things. It wasn't until the late eighteenth and early nineteenth century that it began to be used about piety. The spiritual life was divided into asceticism, which focused on human striving for the many, and mysticism, God's special gift for the few. It is only in the last thirty years or so that the word spirituality has come into common usage. Since then many writers have attempted to define what they see as the present meaning of Christian spirituality.

We can describe our religious experiences as spirituality; reflection on this experience by theologians is also called spirituality. The history of spirituality can be a study of either of these, or of both. In the present century there has been a remarkable development in theological reflection on all kinds of religious experience.

Even within Christian spirituality there is a variety of spiritualities. People will speak about a Marian spirituality, an Ignatian spirituality, a Eucharistic spirituality, a Franciscan spirituality, a spirituality of marriage, or a spirituality of the single life. There are two reasons for this. Firstly, God is transcendent. He cannot be contained by any human category. Secondly, each person seeking a Christian spirituality is different in background, culture, outlook, mentality; new depths and insights are always evolving. In each generation people may seek a new insight or way of living out the gospel.

Central to Christian spiritualities are the love of the Trinity, the Word of God, the person of Jesus Christ, celebrated in the sacraments, especially baptism, confirmation and Eucharist, and lived as church. The way in which these are ordered will determine the type of spirituality, e.g. the Franciscan tradition interprets most of the above through poverty and simplicity; Jesuit spirituality uses the prism of finding God and his will in all things and giving glory to him.

Some Definitions of Spirituality
It might be helpful to give some recent descriptions or attempted definitions of spirituality.
- In 1983 Gordon Wakefield described spirituality as the way in which prayer influences our conduct, our behaviour and manner of life, our attitudes to other people.[1]
- Sandra Schneiders describes spirituality as the experience of

conscious involvement in the project of life-integration through self-transcendence towards the ultimate value one perceives. She goes on to state that in Christian Spirituality this ultimate value is the triune God revealed in Jesus Christ and the project involves the living of his paschal mystery in the context of the church community through the gift of the Holy Spirit.[2]

- Donal Dorr sees the passage of scripture from the Book of Micah as a basis for a balanced spirituality: 'This is what Yahweh asks of you, only this: that you act justly, that you love tenderly, that you walk humbly with your God.' (Micah 6:8)[3]

- Ernest Larkin describes it as a living of the Paschal Mystery which consists in the passage from death to life, sacramentally expressed especially in baptism and the Holy Eucharist and existentially lived in one's daily life.[4]

- Dympna Magee defines spirituality as following where the Spirit leads us in a faith and prayer life, in our own story lived and worked out in the world where we find ourselves – by ourselves and with all those others, near and far who make up our world.[5]

- The Centre for Human Development, based at the Catholic University of America, defines spirituality as a journey of faith on which we are all wounded pilgrims. It is our unique response to God as he reveals himself from moment to moment in the changing textures of life. This response calls into play all aspects of our being.

Common to all of these would seem to be the following – the idea of a search, a journey of life or a way. When we seek to get behind these ideas it is clear that the spirituality will be a personal appropriation of the great command to love God and neighbour (Mt 22:18), to act in faith, hope and charity, to live in the Spirit, sharing the family life of God (Rom 8), a life made possible through the sacraments and guided by the teaching of Jesus and the church. This usually includes, at least implicitly, some idea of self-transcendence. Many spiritualities insist that we 'de-centre' from ourselves and find a new centre for our lives in God, the absolute, the Divine Other and in the love of neighbour that he demands absolutely.

Steps Towards a Lay Spirituality

On the eve of Vatican II the spirituality of the laity mainly consisted in sacramental life, prayers and good works. There was little emphasis on ideas like the Christian life being rooted in baptism. 'Good' Christian laity went to confession weekly or monthly. The Eucharist was seen as a celebration of Calvary and people offered themselves along with Christ the Priest. During the celebration of the Eucharist people were largely passive and concentrated on their own private prayers such as saying the Rosary or novenas. Personal prayer consisted of the Rosary, devotion to the Sacred Heart, Mary and the saints. Generally speaking spirituality and the secular were two poles of people's lives. They said their prayers and then got on with their lives, attempting to be loving and caring as they did so

Schools of Spirituality

Though the Council acknowledged the existence of different spiritualities, it is not so clear how spiritualities differ. In the Constitution on the Church, chapter five and especially in chapter six, along with the decree on Religious Life, *Perfectae caritatis (PC)*, we have several references to spiritual schools or families. Though we can readily recognise the existence of such families, it is not so easy to locate their identity. One frequently hears language which would suggest that if we eliminated what was common to Benedictines, Franciscans and Jesuits we would have something identifiable left that would be specific to Benedictine, Franciscan or Jesuit spirituality. Christopher O'Donnell, the Carmelite theologian, has argued that seeking such a residue is not the way forward. Using rather the analogy of building materials, he suggests that quite different bungalows would be built by three builders all using identical materials. Following this path, O'Donnell suggests that spiritualities are to be sought not in a difference of content but in the emphasis, order, inter-relationship of the same materials. The importance of this insight will emerge when we examine the ways in which writings of the council have described lay spirituality.[7]

When we come to the difficult area of identifying a lay spirituality we can begin with the premise that laity are not called to a second class holiness but to the perfection of charity (*LG* 39) like every other member of the church.

Jesus is the paradigm for ministerial priests and religious discerning their relationship to God, Christ, the church and the world. So too the laity have in Jesus the source for discerning their own orientation to these realities in their lives ... Imitation of Jesus as the disciple of the Father offers to all the Christian faithful a pattern for imitation, a pattern that cannot be, in the light of Vatican II and the New Code, the prerogative of only clergy and religious.[8]

Lay spirituality cannot be seen as something inferior to a religious or clerical spirituality. The challenge of a lay spirituality is to live in the midst of the world, with all its joys and sorrows, and tensions, in the deep realisation that it is here that the laity live out their Christian vocation and grow in holiness, love of God and neighbour

We have already noted the variety of ways in which spirituality itself is understood. The problem is heightened in the case of lay spirituality. When we look at some contemporary writers, we find that though they are reasonably successful in speaking about lay identity, they are not so convincing about lay spirituality. They will generally insist on the elements out of which such spirituality is composed, e.g. scripture, grace, sacraments, prayer. How these are expressed and lived in a lay spirituality is less clear.

- Keith Egan sees lay spirituality as a spirituality of discipleship. Discipleship puts before all Christians the demand that Jesus put to the rich young man (Mt 19:16-30: Mk 10:17-25; Lk 18:18-30). It urges them to accept freely the gift of this call from Jesus (Mk 1:16-20). Discipleship is a call to belong to a community of disciples, in fact, to belong to a new family (Mk 3:20-35), to do what Jesus did – to teach, to heal, to overcome evil – to belong to a community of service. Finally, discipleship calls all Christians to pray as Jesus prayed (Mt 14:26-42), and to follow him into his suffering, death, and resurrection – to die and rise with Jesus (Mk 14: 43; 16: 8).[9]
- Pope John Paul II develops this theme of lay discipleship. He states that the invitation 'go, sell your possessions and give the money to the poor,' and the promise, 'you will have treasure in heaven' are meant for everyone, because they bring

out the full meaning of the commandment of love for neighbour, just as the invitation which follows, 'Come follow me',
is the new, specific form of the commandment of love of
God.[10]

- Ronald Rolheiser speaks of four pillars of lay spirituality
based on Matthew Chapter six: 1) Private prayer and private
morality; 2) Social justice; 3) Mellowness of heart and spirit;
4) Community as a constitutive element of true worship.[11] He
insists that a key consideration must be a balanced spirituality.
It must reflect equilibrium in love of God, ourselves and our
neighbour. It involves living as a full member of the church
community, working for justice in society and the world. It
involves a balanced time given to personal and community
prayer.[12] Rolheiser asserts that spirituality is about 'liberality
and piety, action and contemplation, private morality and
social justice, the concerns of feminism and Greenpeace and
the Ten Commandments. Sadly today – and this is one of our
major stumbling blocks to living a healthy spirituality – these
are invariably divorced from each other.'

- Agnes Cunningham around the time of Vatican II posed the
question, 'Does a lay spirituality exist?' which for her pre-
supposes two other questions. Firstly, she asked if by 'lay
spirituality' one understands a spirituality of the laity or a
spirituality for the laity and, secondly, if it exists, whether it
differs from any other type of spirituality? She concluded
that a spirituality *of* the laity does exist in that the lay person
has been incorporated into the People of God, has been in-
serted into Christ and lives in the Trinity (Rom 5:5) but a spirituality *for* the laity does not exist. Cunningham stresses that
there is no difference between the holiness of the lay person
and the holiness of religious though it differs in its expression, being seen through the 'shape of the vessel it fills.' She
then goes on to use the analogy of plants. The manner in
which each plant takes in water, minerals and air and
changes them into its unique type of beauty will vary. She
concludes that spirituality will always be individualised but
never individualistic.[13]

- Leonard Doohan sees lay spirituality as 'being church in its
fullness.'[14] Through baptism the laity are the church, and are

called to live out the implications of baptism by being at the centre of the church and the centre of the world. As a church community they are called to take an active role in the sacramental and liturgical life of the church. Liturgical celebration flows from the daily experiences of the laity, and influences and strengthens the circumstances of their lives and work in the world. They are called to build the community dimension of church in all aspects of lay life, family, work, at parish, diocesan, national and international level. Flowing from baptism, each person is endowed with charisms for the life and work of the church and filled with gifts of faith, hope and charity. The laity share in the priesthood of all the baptised and in the three-fold office of priest, prophet and king and are therefore called to reach out in mission to the church and the world.

Lay Spirituality, Essential to the Church
The question of lay spirituality is clearly central for the welfare of the church. Associated with, or perhaps included in, the notion of lay spirituality is the issue of community. In some way the way of renewal must necessarily involve community. However, as is clear from the history of the church and Vatican II, renewal is not a matter of mere human initiative. Ultimately it must be a work of the Spirit. Another point which emerges is the importance of evangelisation or mission. Since in some sense the laity's task and mission is in the secular arena, an emphasis on mission will be essential. Finally, in evolving a spirituality for the laity, the church must be concerned not merely in producing what is aesthetically pleasing or satisfying, but rather what must lead to renewed commitment to Christian discipleship and to the task of being truly lay in the church. There is an urgent need for adult catechesis and the formation of the laity in the church. The lack of a determined and sustained programme of adult involvement, education and catechesis is one of the major reasons for the drifting away of people from the church. These five notions of spirituality – community, charism, mission, commitment, formation – are not only crucial for the identity, role and spirituality of the laity today but can be given ever new and attractive expressions. One of these, associate membership of a religious congregation, is the main topic of this book.

We have then a sense of something important emerging in the theology and spirituality of laity to help us grasp the significance of this new situation. The next chapter will outline the progressive marginalisation and neglect of laity, especially in communicating to them the fullness of holiness to which they are called. An outline from the New Testament to the eve of Vatican II will show times of enrichment but more often of poverty in the presentation of, and quest for, lay holiness.

FURTHER READING

Church Documents

Flannery, A., *Vatican Council II: Dogmatic Constitution on the Church (Lumen gentium) 1964*. Revised translation in inclusive language especially Chapter Five,'The Universal Call to Holiness' (Dublin: Dominican Publications, 1996).

The Catechism of the Catholic Church,, 'Christian Holiness,' nos 2012-2016 (Dublin: Veritas Publications, 1994) 438.

Post-Synodal Apostolic Exhortation of John Paul on 'The Vocation and the Mission of the Lay Faithful in the Church and World,' *Christifideles laici*, Chapter One, (London: Catholic Truth Society 1988).

Articles & Books

J. Aumann, *Christian Spirituality in the Catholic Tradition*, (London: Sheed & Ward, 1985).

P. Collins, *Spirituality for the Twenty-First Century: Living in a Secular Age*, (Dublin: Columba Press, 1999).

R. Rolheiser, *Seeking Spirituality: Guidelines for a Christian Spirituality for the Twenty-First Century*, (London: Hodder & Stoughton, 1998).

E. C. Selliner, 'Lay Spirituality,' in *The New Dictionary of Spirituality*, ed M. Downey. (Collegeville: The Liturgical Press, 1993) 589-596.

J. Wolski Conn, 'Spirituality,' in *The New Dictionary of Theology*, eds J. A. Komonchak *et al*, (Collegeville: The Liturgical Press, 1987) 972-986.

NOTES

1. Quoted in *A Dictionary of Christian Spirituality*, (London, SCM, 1983), p v.
2. S. M. Schneiders, 'The Study of Christian Spirituality: Contours and Dynamics of a Discipline,' *Christian Spirituality Bulletin* 6 (1998) 2-12 at 2-3.
3. D. Dorr, 'A Balanced Spirituality,' *Furrow* 34 (1983) 758.
4. E. Larkin, 'The Place of Asceticism in Modern Life,' *Concilium* 9 (1996) 52.
5. D. Magee, 'Laity: A Developing Role,' *Priest and People* 1 (1987) 130.

6. Quoted in M. Morton, 'What Do We Mean by Spirituality?', *Priest and People* 1 (1987) 341.

7. C.O'Donnell, 'Core Marian Themes in the Carmelite Order: Patroness, Mother, Sister, Most Pure Virgin', in *Carmel and Mary: Theology and History of a Devotion*, ed J. Welch, (Washington, The Carmelite Institute, 2002) 67-88 at 81-83.

8. K. J. Egan, 'The Call of the Laity to a Spirituality of Discipleship', *The Jurist* 47, 84-85.

9. Ibid, 84-85.

10. John Paul II, Encyclical, 'The Splendour of Divine Truth,' *Veritatis splendour* (1993) 18.

11. R. Rolheiser, 'The Essential Outline for a Christian Spirituality,' in *Seeking Spirituality: Guidelines for a Christian Spirituality for the Twenty-First Century* (London, Sydney: Hodder & Stoughton, 1998) at 18.

12. Ibid, 52-66.

13. A. Cunningham, 'Complexity and Challenge: The American Catholic Layman,' *Concilium* 9 (1965) 58-65.

14. L. Doohan, 'Critical Issues for the Laity,' *The Way* Supp. 60 (1987) 23-32.

CHAPTER TWO

The Laity from
New Testaments times to the eve of Vatican II

For the Christian community the early church stands always as norm and model. In it we meet the disciples of Jesus beginning, through the Holy Spirit, to develop his vision for the world. Every area of theology and every aspect of church life needs to tap into the early church. Indeed when we say that the church is apostolic, we are perhaps primarily asserting that the church must constantly be faithful to the ideals of the early church.

However, it is not always easy to be sure that the picture we develop of the early church is rounded and authentic. That is partly because of the nature of the New Testament evidence which consists of four types of documents and is concerned with two basic issues. The four kinds of texts are accounts of the life, death and glorification of Jesus (the gospels), an outline history of the early spread of the church (Acts), reflections on the mystery of Christ and the ethical consequences of this mystery in the lives of the community and individuals in the early church (the Letters) and lastly a visionary document that looks to past, present and future in very symbolic language (Revelation). In all this literature there are two crucial issues: Jesus Christ, his personal mission and salvation; and secondly the response of the disciples which is primarily faith and holiness.

The New Testament
Since our concerns are with the laity, we look first at the laity in the New Testament, its twenty-seven documents which were written over a space of about fifty years, beginning with First Thessalonians which we can date with some confidence about 51AD. If we were to summarise the concerns of the New Testament it would be to look at a body of people who are disciples of Jesus, filled by the Holy Spirit, and seeking to live in him and to bring his name to others. In this fascinating period of the

early church, what can one say about the laity? A chief difficulty will be to avoid the anachronism which would be to impose later views on earlier texts and situations. Granted that we do not find the word 'laity' in the New Testament we can, however, find much for our study of the laity and lay spirituality.

Here those who belong to God are those who are baptised and believe in Christ. The disciples of Jesus constitute the new people (*laos*) of God (see 1 Pet 2:9). The *laos* are the chosen people in contrast to the pagans around them. Frequently used New Testament terms are 'the elect' (*eklektoi*), 'the holy ones' (*hagioi*), 'disciples' (*mathetai*) or 'the brothers' (*adelphoi*). Within the New Testament community some members had specific tasks, special charisms and duties. No reference was made to ordained or non-ordained nor to cleric or lay. Christ is the head of the church. All members serve him. The only distinction is between the world and the community members. The Christian life of the community can be summed up in two lines of scripture from the Acts of the Apostles:

> They devoted themselves to the apostles' instruction and the communal life, the breaking of bread and the prayers. (Acts 2:42)

Here we see a Christian community worshipping God, preaching the good news, sharing everything and caring for each other's needs. This was not any haphazard gathering of the community but one based on the apostolic proclamation that Jesus Christ is Lord (1 Cor 12:3). The Eucharist was at the centre of the community which led to love of God in prayer and a reaching out in love to the neighbour. The disciples were faithful in passing on the teaching of the apostles. The Old Testament scriptures were interpreted in the light of the risen Christ. Central to the early Christian church was the proclaiming of the good news. The result of this proclamation was the creation of a community (*koinonia*).

The word *koinonia* is a difficult word to translate in English. Its basic meaning is what is common, from the root Greek word *koin-*. So words such as 'fellowship', 'participation', 'communion' and 'solidarity' express something of the sense of *koinonia*. The Protestant churches use the word 'fellowship' which for them is a warm affective word. The Irish have a word *muintearas* ('communityness'). 'Sharing' and 'what is held in common' are also used to translate this rich word. *Koinonia* has two directions: we have communion/sharing with God, i.e. vertical *koinonia*, and we have communion/sharing with one another, i.e. horizontal *koinonia*. One can also speak of a vertical communion throughout the ages, back to Jesus and the apostolic church.

The New Testament community recognised the church as a community, a *koinonia* which had its source in God through Jesus Christ.

> The whole group of believers was united, heart and soul; no one claimed private ownership of any possessions, as everything they owned was held in common. The apostles continued to testify to the resurrection of the Lord Jesus with great power.' (Acts 4: 32-35)

They were in loving communion with each other (see 1 Jn 13). They found themselves cared for by others. Another characteristic of the early Christian community was the Eucharist. The disciples were faithful to the breaking of bread (Acts 2:42), the sign and symbol of Christian unity. When the early Christians partook of the one loaf, they declared that they were one with each other. It is the bond which marks the Christian community. The breaking of bread was meaningful and fruitful for the early Christian community because they were rooted in the apostles' teaching and were living in loving communion (1 Cor 10:1), and serving one another (*diakonia*). The celebration of Eucharist flows from apostolic *kerygma* (the proclamation of Jesus as Lord) and *koinonia*. The Christian community is a community of worship, mission and service.

A final characteristic of the early Christian community as stated in Acts 2:42 was that they were devoted to prayer. Their prayer was very much centred on the psalms (see Acts 4:23-26). They also prayed prayers of praise and thanksgiving. Prayers of intercession too played a large part in their prayer even to the extent of offering their own sufferings for the spreading of the good news (see 1 Thess 1:2-5; 2 Cor 6:4-6).

The text of Acts 2:42-47 speaks of enthusiasm, joy, prayer and sharing. We see an early community that freely praised God while giving a clear witness to an alternative way of living. At the centre of their lives was love of God and neighbour. They were ready to suffer martyrdom for the sake of the gospel.

The Early Centuries

The ideal vision of the New Testament (see Acts 2:42-47; 4:32-35; 5:12-16), was gradually to give way to two distinct groups within the church, namely the hierarchy and the laity. The earliest reference to the terms lay and cleric is found in *The Letter of Clement* at the end of the first century: 'the layman is bound by the ordinances of the laity.' At the beginning of the third century, the terms lay and cleric begin to signify distinct categories among the people. The lay person is now described negatively as non-cleric.[1] Throughout the third and following centuries the laity became more and more passive and played little role in the affairs of the church except for their active duty of contributing money for the support of the clergy and of those poor assisted by the bishop. Women were never called laity, probably because they generally did not have the money to play this key lay role.

By the fifth century the presbyters were undertaking all ministries, except those relating to financial support. The clericalisation of almost all ministries accounted for the diminished status of the lay person. With the growth of monasticism, the pecking order was clergy, monks and laity. The laity were those who were not clergy or religious. Gratian (ca 1159), the Father of Canon Law, in a simplistic way stated:

'There are two kinds of Christians, clerics and lay people.'[2]

The relationship between church and state deteriorated after 1050. Disputes about church property and lay investiture furthered the division between clergy and laity during the reign of Gregory VII (1073-1085). He claimed as pope to have the right to dispense with oaths of allegiance and as spiritual ruler to be superior to kings and princes. There was to be little change in this distinction of clergy and laity up to Vatican II (1962-1965).

Up to the time of Constantine, we have in general a continuation of the New Testament approach. Gradually, however, we find a specialised literature addressed to specific groups within the church, such as those preparing for martyrdom, widows, virgins, clergy. Here the determining element was their state or circumstances, rather than the basic fact that they were Christians.

Already in this chapter we have seen the gradual evolution of the laity and the issues concerning their identity. But though we have seen that the laity emerge as an identifiable group within the church, a spirituality for them did not develop. Indeed there were three influences of the first millennium that would impact quite negatively on lay spirituality or be a blockage to its emergence. These were the development of

- dualistic heresies such as gnosticism, manicheism, montanism
- monasticism
- the clerical and lay divide.

Heresies

During the second and third centuries there were many heresies. Though not fully clear in all aspects, some of them appear to have had dualistic tendencies, holding matter in some sense to be evil. These represent fairly permanent or universal patterns of thought so that, if we are not careful, we can find traces of them in ourselves and in our society even today. People did not set out to be wrong. The church was seeking to articulate at other times and places the revelation which came to it from a Jewish culture. The struggle to express the truth is found in every area of theology. Thus we find the great creeds which expressed the truth about Jesus Christ and about the Holy Trinity. Those who refused to accept these were loosely called heretics. From our point of view there were heresies which would indirectly influence the development of spirituality, especially lay spirituality.[3]

These heresies were to be particularly troublesome and, as we said, likely to recur. Gnostism, from the Greek word knowledge, offers special revelation, secret truths, or wisdom, apart from Christian revelation and tradition. Some contemporary New Age spiritualities seem Gnostic. Manicheism is an extreme form which sees two ultimate conflicting principles of good and evil. Contemporary spirituality and politics are not free from traces of Manicheism in phrases such as 'empires of evil' (George Bush). The third heresy, Montanism, was an exaggerated

enthusiasm for spiritual things to the neglect or rejection of institutes and sacraments.

Marginalisation

With the ending of the persecutions, a substitute was found for
martyrdom as an expression of total dedication. The early
Christians believed that great suffering, especially martyrdom,
showed one's commitment to the Lord and the power of Christ's
presence. A spirituality that allowed them to suffer to the point
of death rather than turn away from the Lord became a model
for all. Cyprian of Carthage (ca 200-258), Polycarp (ca 69-155)
and Ignatius of Antioch (d ca 107) were very much influenced
by this attitude. Ignatius of Antioch believed, at least for himself,
that perfection and martyrdom were synonymous. The martyr
is the perfect disciple of Christ (see Mt 10:38; 16:24; Lk 14-26).

With the passing of the persecutions, the death of the body
became spiritualised. Virginity, and later asceticism, were seen
as giving one's life for Christ. It would later be called 'white
martyrdom'. St Paul already gave the eschatological reason for
virginity when he spoke of the end of the world (see 1 Cor 7:25-
31). At first St Paul and the early church believed that the second
coming of Christ was imminent and they lived as if the church
was already in the last days.[4]

Those who wished to give themselves fully to God would
first choose martyrdom, and if this was not possible, they would
join the monastic life which emphasised flight from the world
and celibacy or virginity. Men and women fled into the deserts
of Syria, Egypt and Palestine to show their love for God through
prayer, fasting, and severe mortification of the body. The ideal
for spirituality became mainly monastic. Gregory Nazianzus (d
389) said, 'The contemplative life is for those few who are perfect, the active life is for everyone else.' Forms of prayer,
penances, a negative approach to matter and the body and the
depreciation of marriage were imposed on the laity. All of this
held back any possible development of a lay spirituality.[5]

The most serious negative influence was the isolation of lay
people from administration and liturgy. In the Middle Ages we
can accurately speak of a clerical/lay divide. In the early centuries the distinction between clergy and laity had widened, with

the laity seen in negative terms and as having a passive role in liturgy. Their main task, as we have seen, was to support the clergy financially so that the clergy could dedicate themselves to worship, the administration of the sacraments and to prayer. Noteworthy in the late sixth and early seventh centuries, during the pontificate of Pope Saint Gregory (590-604), was the identification of two classes of laity. These were the ordinary laity and then the more fervent or devout. This state of affairs would continue right into the Middle Ages.

Late Middle Ages
By the Middle Ages society had become very stratified. One could see two sectors in society – the clergy and laity. But lay life had its own layers – nobility, merchants, peasants and many more divisions. Very few could read and write, apart from the nobility and merchants, though many of the latter had functional literacy only: they could read and write about business but might not be able to read the New Testament. Up to the twelfth century, books on spirituality were written mostly by monks.

By the late Middle Ages the ordinary laity before their baptism received a basic instruction on the duties of Christians and were prepared for marriage. More 'devout' Christians usually grouped themselves around the churches or monasteries and led a penitential life. They attended the Divine Office in the monastery, had private prayer and lived a life of austerity. A vow of celibacy became common among unmarried laity.

In time, the monasteries developed and became centres of civilisation. This was even before the development of urban civilisation about the eleventh century. As they grew richer, many monasteries fell away from their gospel ideals. However, in France with the founding of the Camaldolese, Carthusian and Cistercian orders, and through reforms associated with the abbeys of Cluny and Bec, monastic spirituality was renewed in the eleventh and twelfth centuries. Many of these orders welcomed laity. Many lay men and women placed themselves at the service of the monks almost as servants. They were known as *conversi* or *sorores* because their motivation was frequently conversion. Often the monks of Cluny accepted lay people into the order through the profession of vows and then buried them in the religious habit as a guarantee of salvation.

Towards the middle of the twelfth century lay people as well as clerics began to claim the vision of the apostolic life for themselves. A new phenomenon arose, namely the mystics. A significant number of the great mystics were women and lay, who communicated their experiences not in the Latin language of the schools but in the newly emerging vernaculars such as early forms of Germanic and Romance Languages. Such mystical writing, often coming from the laity, mystical women and in the vernacular languages, was not well received by the clerical classes and partly led to what Hans Urs von Balthasar and Karl Rahner have described as a disastrous split between spirituality and theology.

A new and strongly lay understanding of discipleship was more and more stressed. It emphasised radical poverty; itinerant preaching also emerged. At this time we find in the Low Countries the Beguines and Beghards, lay movements of the twelfth and thirteenth centuries that advocated a simple lifestyle, ordinary work and communities of friends.[6]

Some of these lay movements were critical of and antagonistic to features of the institutional church, especially its power and wealth. These criticisms were often crudely expressed and were dismissed out of hand by churchmen. Therefore lay movements somewhat paradoxically can be seen to have increased the isolation of the laity.

From the fourteenth century, an enormous literature of prayers, legends, and pious exercises developed. A very important movement in spirituality, called the 'New Devotion' (*Devotio moderna*) emerged and was centred in the Low Countries. It reacted to very abstract and complex mystical writing and it sought a practical spirituality. It advocated an educated laity, daily meditation, a vital liturgical life and the need for spiritual guides. An increase in the use of the vernacular made some writings more available to the laity. Perhaps the most famous advocate of *Devotio moderna* was Thomas à Kempis (1379-1471). He is credited with writing *The Imitation of Christ*, a book extremely popular up to Vatican II, and a favourite of St Thérèse of Lisieux. It can be seen as an attempt to make spirituality accessible to everyone.

The church from the Fourth Lateran Council (1215) to the

Council of Trent (1545-1563) became more and more hierarchical. A pyramidal vision of the church evolved in place of the
communio New Testament vision. Under Pope Bonface VIII this
development reached its climax when he declared that Christ
gave both spiritual and temporal power to the pope. In 1296
Boniface declared that the laity were sworn enemies of the clergy.
Given this background, it is not hard to understand how anti-
clerical movements arose. The laity became very much second-
rate members of the church, were passive liturgically and waited
to be ministered to by the clergy. Any participation in church
affairs, or active lay involvement in councils, was almost non-
existent. There was to be little change in this institutional divide
between clergy and laity up to the Second Vatican Council
(1962-1965).

Sixteenth and Seventeenth Centuries
The sixteenth century was a time of great turmoil for the church
and also a time of rich spirituality. Some very gifted people like
Martin Luther and John Calvin saw the church in need of radical
reform. At some levels the church was slow to answer the profound challenges of the Reformation. We had, for example, to
wait until Vatican II for a vernacular liturgy and the restoration
of communion from the cup. The movement of reformers was
very much a lay movement, focused on lay princes and nobles
with peasant farmers, shopkeepers or tradesmen. But the impe-
tus of reformation, and the Catholic reaction called the 'Counter
Reformation', witnessed one of the greatest explosions of spirituality in the history of the church. From the time of the
Reformation there was a certain fear of laity and anything that
would smack of democracy. Since Martin Luther emphasised
the priesthood of the laity, it remained undeveloped by Catholic
theologians.

The church in the second millennium became what Yves
Congar would later call a hierarchology. But the story is not to
be told only in dark tones. There were extremely important figures for lay spirituality. One was St Ignatius Loyola (1491-1556).
His influence down through the centuries on lay spirituality has
been remarkable. He was a soldier before his conversion and
was very aware of the laity and the need for a balance between

prayer and service. He made two outstanding contributions to spirituality. Firstly, he gave the church a new form of religious life by sending religious into the world to preach the gospel. Secondly, he produced his *Spiritual Exercises* primarily for lay people to enable them discern the direction of their lives and to help them to recommit themselves to Christ.[7] For those lay people who were too busy to set aside a month for the exercises he provided the nineteenth note or annotation allowing them to complete the exercises over a period of time. His advice to lay people was to seek God in all things. He saw all life as holy, whether it was religious, clerical or lay. His was to be a most influential and successful attempt to give an integrated view of the Christian life in the world.

Another man, Saint Francis de Sales (1562-1622) was very involved in the Counter-Reformation. Before becoming Bishop of Geneva (Calvin's home) he had wide experience in school and university circles. He was influenced by St Ignatius and did much to advocate a spirituality of the laity in his book *Introduction to the Devout Life*. He is perhaps the best known of the pioneers in composing a treatise on lay spirituality. He states in his *Introduction*:

> I want to teach people who live in crowded cities within their families, in the middle of domestic cares at home or in the press of public affairs in their professional life ... It's a mistake, even a heresy, to want to banish the devout life from the soldier's camp, the manual worker's workshop, the court of princes, the homes of married people.

A great contribution of Francis de Sales to spirituality was that he brought morality and holiness under the one umbrella of love and returned in an urgent way to the spirituality of the New Testament and the universal call to holiness. For him, Christian perfection does not come from any particular exercise or practice but is to be found in the love of God and neighbour and is the vocation of all Christians, whether they are cleric, religious or lay. He has been called the 'father of modern spirituality.'[8]

French School
Another development which would be enormously important arose in France, a school or movement of spirituality which was

deeply influenced by the Spanish mystics. Though it involved more clergy than laity it would have a significance directly and indirectly for lay spirituality. A key figure was Cardinal Pierre de Bérulle (1575-1629) who made a profound contribution to spirituality.[9] He in turn had been influenced by St Ignatius and St Francis de Sales and especially by the salon of Madame Acarie. Here a group of Christians gathered regularly, including the young Bérulle. They presented holiness as accessible to everyone. What was necessary for holiness was adherence to the will of God as discovered in one's life. As Jesus had to come to his passion and death to follow the will of the Father, so must the Christian be reduced to 'nothingness' in order to move towards union with God.

A spirituality centred on Christ was the chief characteristic of Bérulle's spirituality. His main theme was that through the incarnation of Jesus all human life, and human states corrupted and tainted by the sin of Adam and Eve, have been deified in the three states (*états*) of Jesus:

- his state as the Second Person of the Holy Trinity – both God and man;
- his state of infancy;
- his Eucharistic state.

Spiritual infancy was the theme of the French School and continued into the nineteenth century, reaching its highest peak in Saint Thérèse of Lisieux (The Little Flower, 1873-1897) in her very well known 'Little Way'.

Bérulle also brought about a renewal in devotion to Mary, always seeing Mary in her relationship with Jesus and Jesus' relationship with Mary.

Medieval Schools

We have already alluded to schools of spirituality in the previous chapter. After the Reformation there was a revitalisation in the Benedictine family as well as in the mendicant orders, Augustinians, Carmelites, Dominicans and Franciscans. We find members of these orders writing books of piety and treatises on the virtues specifically for laity.

Among the Dominican school of spirituality, Louis of

Granada advocated the universal call of all Christians to holiness and the perfection of charity, a theme which would later be taken up by the Second Vatican Council. He preached and wrote mainly for the laity, because he believed that they were called to the fullness of the Christian life.[10] In the Carmelite school of spirituality, St Teresa of Avila (1515-1582) and St John of the Cross (1542-1591) have given a spiritual doctrine to the church which has been extraordinarily influential.[11] What was important to Carmelite spirituality was purity of heart. If the deepest core of a person's being is centred on God, then it is of secondary importance whether a person is a religious, priest or lay person. According to St Teresa of Avila, God can be found among the pots and pans. St John of the Cross writes of the spiritual life as a journey in faith and love.

Modern Heresies

We have seen earlier three heretical movements in the first millennium that presented dangers to those seeking the way of God. Towards the end of the seventeenth century we find three more deviant movements. Even though we do not find these heretical tendencies in their pure state after the eighteenth century, traces of them can still be found in contemporary spirituality and in people's lives. They were Illuminism, Quietism and Jansenism.

Illuminism

Illuminism was a lay movement which originated in the first quarter of sixteenth-century Spain. Those following illuministic tendencies advocated a spirituality where they felt there was little need for the institutional church, the sacraments or for use of the will or intellect. They felt rather that by abandoning themselves in total passivity to the Holy Spirit, they received interior enlightenment, illumination. They were thus known as the Illuminists (*Alumbrados*). One of the chief advocates of this quietist spirituality was Juan de Valdés. Illuminism led to much distrust of spirituality on the part of church authorities. It spread from Spain to France and Italy. It was condemned in 1529 but continued to develop alongside, and found its fullest expression in, the Quietist movement.

Quietism

Quietism, again, stressed complete and total passivity before God. Union with him was achieved by abandoning the intellect and will and one's self completely to God in non-discursive meditative prayer. No other forms of prayer or of self-mortification were allowed. It was advocated by Michael Molinos (1628-1698) in Spain, and in France Fénelon was accused of it, though he was not a close follower of the extreme quietism of the lay woman Madame Guyon (d 1717). Controversy in France led to a distrust of mystical literature which lasted nearly two centuries.

Jansenism

Jansenism arose in the University of Louvain and spread to France through the meeting of two students, Cornelius Jansen (d 1643) and Jean Duvergier de Hauranne. Jansenism presented extreme views in the area of grace. It developed after Jansen's death but was based on his harsh ideas. Janenism held that because of original sin humanity had lost free choice and could not resist temptation. It had a very poor image of humanity and the role of human effort, and a great awe for God. It believed totally in the people's need for God's grace and in their inability to dispose themselves for it. It held that only the very holy and worthy should ever receive Holy Communion. It played down the humanity of Jesus and did not hold that Jesus died for all. Jansenism led to much scrupulosity. It was condemned in 1654 by Pope Innocent X and the succeeding popes, Clement and Pius VI. Jansenism lingered into the twentieth century and led often to a great sense of unworthiness among people in their relationship with God, keeping them from assuming their proper role in the mission of the church.

These three movements, Illuminism, Quietism and Jansenism, had a profound effect on the church; mystical and the classical texts would be little read in eighteenth century Europe, apart from Germany.

One could remark in passing that the attitude of Reformation churches varied in the seventeenth and eighteenth centuries. On the one hand, access to scripture and *The Book of Common Prayer* opened the way for deeper piety amongst the laity. But although there was profound spirituality in the Anglican poets and some divines, it would only be with Wesley that a popular spirituality arose in Britain. With John and Charles Wesley too we find a rich treasury of magnificent hymns which sustained an evangelical spirituality among the laity.

Eighteenth and Nineteenth Centuries

In eighteenth and nineteenth century England the works of Bishop R. Challoner, Father Faber, the two cardinals, Manning and Newman, cannot be overlooked in a study of lay spirituality. Challoner's publication, *The Garden of the Soul* (1740), was intended as a book of spiritual exercises and instructions for lay people and aimed 'to bring devotion out of the cloister into the world'. Fr Faber produced a large quantity of spiritual literature and hymns but he lacked the genius of the Wesleys in combining verse, theology and spirituality. Faber's influence was rather Italianate. His fellow Oratorian Newman, coming from an Anglican background and with a highly crafted sense of English style, wrote in an entirely different genre. He was acutely aware of the place of the laity. Further he emphasised the relationship between daily life, toil and prayer. In his sermon, 'Doing Glory to God in pursuits of the world,' he encouraged the believer to see Christ as a 'sacrament' through the ordinary activities of the day. In 1859 Newman wrote an article, *On Consulting the Faithful in Matters of Doctrine*, in which he made a strong plea for the education of the Catholic laity. This article was not well received by Rome. Mgr Talbot, representative of the English bishops in Rome, called him the 'most dangerous man in England.' He warned:

> If a check be not placed on the laity in England, they will be rulers of the Catholic Church. What is the province of the laity? To hunt, to shoot, to entertain. These matters they understand. But to meddle with ecclesiastical affairs, they have no right at all.[12]

In Ireland there was a strong tradition of spirituality in the Irish language and a remarkable collection of Irish religious poetry. The Penal Times meant that little of this was published until the late eighteenth century. This spirituality was genuinely of the people and showed a profound integration of faith, spirituality and daily living.[13]

In the nineteenth century, Europe saw the foundation of numerous religious congregations. These were often at first lay developments, with a group of people associating together to respond to particular needs, e.g. Catherine McAuley who worked with other lay people to alleviate poverty and destitution in Dublin. In the case of the Belgian Congregation, the Daughters of Mary and Joseph, of which I am an Associate, Colette de Brandt, a lay woman, was chosen by Father Constant van Crombrugghe, the Founder, as 'superior' of his first community founded to educate poor girls of the area. It was from her that the sisters received direction for their lives though she herself never lived in community with them. Similarly van Crombrugghe, as a young curate in Mouscron, came in contact with a group of lay people under the leadership of Marie Dal. This group originated back in the 1630s and were responsible for the catechesis of the religious foundation, the Daughters of Mary and Joseph, (*Les Filles de Marie et de Joseph*). These groups only became religious congregations when they sought ecclesiastical approval.

Finally, before moving on to the teaching of the Second Vatican Council on the role and identity of the lay person, it is necessary to take a brief look at the identity of the laity in the 1917 Code of Canon Law in order to understand what the church was like when the council opened.

Code of Canon Law (1917)

The Code of Canon Law was an orderly presentation of church law in all its aspects. Up to 1917 there were many collections of laws, often obscure and indeed contradictory. Canon lawyers, bishops and popes decided on particular interpretations in the canonical tradition. Under Pius X (1903-1914) enormous work was undertaken to produce a single compact, ordered and clear presentation of church law. This was promulgated by his successor Benedict XV (1914-1922).

A proper definition of the laity cannot be found in the 1917 Code of Canon Law. The role and function of the laity were known only in contrast to the role and function of the clergy. The Code's attention was focused upon legislating for and about the clergy; the role of the laity then fell into place with reference to the clergy. There are key Canons for an appreciation of the code's view of laity.

Canon 87 states that by baptism a human being becomes a person in the church of Christ, with all the rights and duties of a Christian. There is no mention in this canon of a distinction between lay and cleric. Canon 107 states that:

> By divine institution there are in the church clergy distinct from laity, although not all degrees of clerics are of divine institution. Both clerics and laity may be religious.

One could get the impression that, for the Code, the laity are passive, docile and uneducated. The church is an unequal society and determines the distribution of power between clerics and laity. The clergy and laity are separate and distinct groups in the church, further set apart by clerical dress (Canon 683).

Canon 948 states:

> By the institution of Christ, orders distinguishes clerics from laity in the church for governing the faithful and for the ministry of divine worship.

The 1917 Code of Canon Law lacked an understanding and appreciation of the true interrelationship between clergy and laity. They were described in terms of what each group could or could not do. The laity were passive, the clergy active. The laity were seen negatively as non-clerics. One gets the impression that everything in the church was concentrated in the hierarchy and that there is an excessive concern with power and authority. The laity are seldom mentioned and when they are, the inference is that they are purely passive members of the church, receiving from priests and bishops. Their active participation in the community of the faithful and in the mission of the church was for all practical purposes totally ignored.

With the 1917 Code of Canon Law we come to an end of a process of clericalisation of the church which had begun in the third and fourth centuries. The spirituality of ancient and more recent congregations did not really impinge greatly on the laity except for some prayers and special devotions to saints from religious congregations like Saint Anthony of Padua or Saint Frances of Assisi. There was, however, amongst the laity, a strong devotional life focused on the Blessed Virgin Mary.

Partial development of lay spirituality

It is easy to note the marginalisation of the laity up to Vatican II. We have noted various figures and books that directly addressed the issue of lay spirituality. Some, like the classic work of Frances De Sales, *Introduction to the Devout Life*, attempted some integrity in presenting a challenging spirituality to lay people in whatever state of life they were.

However, one is left with the image of crumbs from rich men's tables. People in rural areas and in towns learned spirituality often by chance encounters. Parish missions, popular from the eighteenth century, might present a Franciscan spirituality one year and five years later, Redemporist, to be followed at five yearly intervals by Jesuit, Vincentian or Passionist spiritualities. Each of these would make their own contribution. Parish mission preaching was very often conversion preaching, to bring people to confession and a return to the sacraments. The preaching often focused on the four last things, death, judgement, hell and heaven. It did not offer much deep spirituality. Some people who lived close to a religious house might have a more integral spirituality, taught and caught from the lives and preaching of the religious. Some orders, as we shall see in a later chapter, had confraternities and third orders which presented a more integral spirituality.

Hence, in looking back over eighteen hundred years, we can see that the communication of spirituality to lay people was frequently haphazard, depending on encounters at parish missions and occasionally by deeply spiritual or charismatic local clergy. It is such a lack of wholeness and the absence of inherited wisdom from religious congregations that left the laity frequently with partial or distorted or unbalanced patterns in their spiritual lives.

This question of wholeness or balance allows us to anticipate the importance of the new development of lay associate membership of a religious congregation.

FURTHER READING

Books & Articles

L. Bouyer et al., *A History of Christian Spirituality*, 3 vols (London: Bums & Oates, 1968).

Y. Congar, *Lay People in the Church* (London: Chapman, 1964). This classic study originally appeared in French in 1951. Many of its insights appear in Vatican II.

K. Kavanaugh & O. Rodriguez, *St Teresa of Avila, Collected Works*, 3 vols (Washington: Institute of Carmelite Studies, 1970-1992).

K. Kavanaugh & O. Rodriguez, *St John of the Cross, Collected Works*, (Washington: Institute of Carmelite Studies, 1979).

D. Orsuto, 'Lay Spirituality' *New Catholic Encyclopedia* (Detroit, Washington, Catholic University of America, 2nd edition. 2003).

L. J. Puhl, *The Spiritual Exercises of St Ignatius* (Chicago: Loyola University Press).

The Study of Spirituality, ed C. Jones, C. Wainwright, E. Yamold, (London: SPCK, 1992). Essays on second millennium, pp 283-473.

J. Gaudemet, 'Les laics dans les premiers siècles de 1' Eglise', *Communio*, (French) 12/1 (1987).

R. Goldie, 'Lay, Laity, Laicity: A Bibliographical Survey of Three Decades,' *The Laity Today* 26 (1979).

C. O'Donnell, 'Laity', *Ecclesia: A Theological Encyclopedia of the Church,* (Collegeville, Minnesota : The Liturgical Press, 1996).

NOTES

1. Congar, 'Laïc et Laïcat,' *Dictionnaire de spiritualité,* (1975) 9: 103.

2. J. Hervada, 'La definicion nominal de laico', *Ius canonicum* 2 (1968) 471-533 in *Canon Law Abstracts* 23 (1969-1970) at 31

3. For first millennium see D. Christie-Murray, *A History of Heresy* (Oxford: University Press, 1989) 1-95

4. See A. Auer, *Open to the World: An Analysis of Lay Spirituality,* (Baltimore: Helicon Press, 1966) at 23

6. See R. Woods, 'Who were the Beguines? The Spirituality of the Lay Reform Movement,' *Spirituality* 4 (1998) 355-358; op. cit. *Spirituality*, 5 26-38

7. See M. Ivens, 'Ignatius Loyola,' in *The Study of Spirituality*, 357-362.

8. See E. Stopp. 'François de Sales' in *The Study of Spirituality*, 379-385.

9. See J. Saward, 'Bérulle and the French School,' in *The Study of Spirituality*, 386-396

1O. See A. Trancho, *Summa of the Christian Life: Selected Texts from the Writings of Venerable Louis Of Granada*, 3 Vols, translated & adapted by J. Aumann (St Louis: B. Herder Books, 1954).

11. See E. W. Trueman Dicken, 'Teresa of Jesus and John of the Cross,' in *The Study of Spirituality*, 363-376; see also H. D. Egan, 'St Teresa of Avila' in *Christian Mysticism: The Future of a Tradition*, 164, (New York:

Pueblo Publishing Company, 1984) 118-164 ; 'St John of the Cross', 165-214.
12. Cited in S. Fagan, 'The Laity: Our Sleeping Giant', *Doctrine and Life* 37 (1987) 2-11 at 2.
12. Peter O' Dwyer, Towards a History of Irish Spirituality (Dublin: The Columba Press, 1995).

CHAPTER THREE

The Laity at Vatican II and after

In the last chapter we have seen the canonical identity of the lay person as being neither clerical nor religious. The twentieth century will see a Copernican revolution in matters of spirituality and the laity.

We are impressed with the novelty and breath of vision at Vatican II (1962-1965). The council did not spring from nowhere. There were developments in theology and in the church, most noticeably after World War One, which prepared the way. Several of these renewal movements directly touched the laity and are important in the development of lay spirituality. These were threefold: firstly, the liturgical movement, secondly, Catholic Action and thirdly, the exploration of the idea of the Mystical Body of Christ. These three, and other developments, paved the way for the Second Vatican Council.

The Liturgical Movement

The Liturgical Movement began in monasteries and academic circles where people published and edited ancient liturgies. This later led to reform in liturgical practice in the nineteenth century and the early twentieth century.[1] Pius X saw the active participation of the people in the liturgy as the centre of the Christian life and the chief source of renewal. Earlier he brought about reforms in Gregorian chant, in the Divine office, daily Communion and lowering the age of First Communion.

The Liturgical Movement continued to have support from Pius XI who produced decrees on the dialogue Mass, on vestments and on chant. In 1947 Pius XII wrote his great encyclical, *Mediator Dei*, which encouraged the active participation of the people in the liturgy, an idea which, as we have seen, had already been suggested by Pius X. He taught that the laity offer the Mass in union with the priest by reason of their own particular share in Christ's priesthood which comes to them through baptism.

Catholic Action

The Liturgical Movement, together with the Catholic Action Movement, were important factors in the re-discovery in the church of the idea of Body and People. This would later give rise to the Vatican II adoption of the term communion (*communio*). Catholic Action did much to develop the idea that the church is not only the institution but is made up of people whom God calls and who respond to his call. The fore runners of Catholic Action were, perhaps, The Society for the Propagation of the Faith, founded by Pauline Jaricot (1799-1862) and The Society of St Vincent de Paul, a charitable organisation to help the poor and needy, founded by Frederick Ozanam (1813-1853). The Society of St Vincent de Paul is still held in high renown and continues to do wonderful work.

Catholic Action can broadly be defined as any activity, on the part of the laity, which is apostolic. A key notion of Catholic Action found in in Mediterranean countries was, however, that it was dependent on the hierarchy, under its direction and sharing in its mission; it was collaboration with the hierarchy. Again, the Popes Pius X, Pius XI and Pius XII, were all involved in calling the laity to Catholic Action. It was Pius XI who has been named the Pope of Catholic Action because of his many writings and addresses on the subject. Early in his pontificate Pope Pius XI in his encyclical, *Ubi arcano* (1922) called the lay apostolate to life. He described Catholic Action as the participation of the laity in the apostolate of the hierarchy. The laity were now seen to share in the apostolate, not so much in virtue of their baptism but as a mandate from the clergy. These two movements, the Liturgical Movement and Catholic Action, linked with the rediscovery of the idea of the Mystical Body, lay behind much of the thinking in ecclesiological circles at the beginning of the Second Vatican Council.

The Mystical Body

In theology the place of the church was newly explored from the

1920s. Previous to that decade ecclesiology had been reflecting on the achievements of Vatican I, which were mostly concerned with the papacy. We know that Vatican I concluded before it could deal with other issues of the church. From the 1920s on, scholars drawing from scripture and tradition began to look at the church in a fresh way. The papal teaching of Pius XII would build on important ideas about the Mystical Body which had been developing before World War II. His encyclical on this topic (*Mystici Corporis,* 1943) in some ways opened paths that Vatican II would explore. In this document he gave a biblical, theological and pastoral understanding of the church as the Mystical Body of Christ and of the mystical union which the members of the church have with one another and with Christ. The church is a body; the church is the Body of Christ; the church is the Mystical Body. A central passage of the Encyclical, which is not very accessible today, is worth quoting at length.

If we would define and describe this true church of Jesus Christ which is the one, holy, catholic, apostolic, Roman Church we shall find nothing more noble, more sublime, or more divine than the expression 'the Mystical Body of Jesus Christ,' an expression that springs from and is, as it were, the fair flowering of the repeated teaching of the Sacred Scriptures and the holy Fathers ... When the Fathers of the Church sing the praises of this Mystical Body of Christ ... they are thinking not only of those who have received holy orders, but all those who, following the evangelical councils, pass their lives either actively among men or hidden in the silence of the cloister or who aim at combining the active and contemplative life according to their institutes; as also of those who, through living in the world, consecrate themselves wholeheartedly to spiritual and corporal works of mercy, and of those who live in the state of matrimony. Indeed, let it be clearly understood, especially in these our days: fathers and mothers of families, those who are godparents through baptism, and in particular those members of the laity who collaborate with the ecclesiastical hierarchy in spreading the kingdom of the divine Redeemer, occupy an honourable, if often a lowly place in the Christian community, and even they, under the impulse of God and with his help, can reach the heights of supreme holiness which, Jesus Christ has promised, will never be wanting to the church.[2]

Mystici Corporis, though it did not use the term 'people of God', did much to revitalise the concept of the church as a body of all the baptised united to Christ, the Head of the Body, and to each other. In this Body every Christian, lay and cleric alike, has a function to fulfill as a participant in the total mission of the church.

At the Second World Congress of the Lay Apostolate in 1957 Pius XII reaffirmed that the sacraments were the basis for the laity's participation in the life of the church which not come as a mandate from the hierarchy as previously held in Catholic Action circles. He also spoke of 'consecration of the world' as an important notion for the laity. In subsequent years the notion of the church as the 'people of God' continued to be developed by Protestant and Catholic theologians, giving a more positive and greater potential for ecumenical developments as compared with the image of the church in *Mystici Corporis*.

Two other people and movements of importance in developing a lay Christian apostolate are worthy of note. In 1928 Saint Josemaría Escrivá laid the foundations for Opus Dei, which received canonical recognition in 1941, becoming a secular institute in 1950. The founder was at pains to develop a genuine lay spirituality for its members. Another important figure was the Belgian priest Joseph Cardijn (1882-1967), founder of the young Christian Workers (YCW). Cardijn devoted his life to the working classes, especially young Christian workers. He sought to bring the workers to an understanding of the importance of their everyday life and their spiritual life, the interconnection between them, and of their call to transform the family, the workplace and the marketplace through their Christian witness and actions. His threefold injunction, 'see, judge, act' became a strategy for many lay movements in the church. The ideals of these two men – and one could cite others – were part of the ferment of ideas in the decades preceding Vatican II. They would be developed later by Vatican II and other documents issued after the council.

Some Theologians

A number of key theologians were to play a leading role in the understanding of lay identity in this pre-Vatican II period. They were Karl Rahner (1904-1984), Gérard Philips (1899-1972), Yves Congar (1904-1995), and Edward Schillebeeckx (1914-).

Yves Congar's publication in 1953 of *Jalons pour une théologie du laïcat* played a key role in the renewal of a theology of the laity. Revised editions with some additions were published in English in 1957 and 1965 respectively, under the title *Lay People in the Church*. Congar wrote this book to do away with the idea that spiritual things belonged solely to the clergy and temporal things to the laity. All laity, religious and clergy alike, participate in the three-fold office of Christ: priest, prophet and king. The laity are called to serve God in the world.

The distinctive element of the vocation and mission of the laity is its secular nature. The church is the whole People of God, clergy and laity alike, the clergy fulfilling their mission in the church and the laity in the world. He thus paved the way for the thinking of Vatican II.

Karl Rahner also made important contributions. He believed that the status of the laity in the church was defined by their specific task in the world and towards the world. However, he warned against the danger of defining the laity solely from their position in the world because they also belong to the church through baptism and confirmation. Rahner saw the mission of the laity flowing from a sacramental identity. However, he believed that only those who exercised an apostolate in ordinary human conditions could be considered laity. Once a person took on a full time ministry in the church, such as catechist, sacristan, or priest's housekeeper, they were no longer members of the laity. According to him, even Catholic Action did not fit into the category of the lay apostolate. This view of the young Rahner was strongly contested by Congar, Phillips, and Schillebeeckx.

Gérard Phillips insisted on the lay status of members of Catholic Action and stressed that there were not two kinds of apostolate as advocated by Rahner, one stemming from the ecclesial church and the other from the ordinary needs of the people. He was a main author of the Constitution on the Church, *Lumen gentium*.

Edward Schillebeeckx again stressed the sacramental foundation, especially baptism and confirmation, for the identity and role of the lay person in the church. Baptism initiates the lay person into the church and into the mission of the church but confirmation is necessary to empower the lay person for the apostolate.

Thus at the beginning of the Second Vatican Council, the vocation and mission of the laity, seen as flowing from their sacramental identity, was theologically mature, as was the term 'people of God'. 'People of God' did not figure much in the first drafts of the Church Constitution, which rather proposed an ecclesiology based on the Mystical Body, with the idea of the Perfect Society also present.

In the decades preceding Vatican II there was an emerging awareness of the mission, therefore, of the laity in the church and the world. What was still needed was a spirituality that would underpin this vision and challenge renewal.

Vatican II

In the twentieth century there were discussions during the pontificates of Pius XI and Pius XII about the advisability of re-convoking Vatican I, which had ceased without being formally closed at the outbreak of the Franco Prussian war (1871). During the late 1940s a lot of material was gathered in great secrecy. The idea of re-convoking Vatican I or calling a new council, however, came to nothing. Pope John XXIII decided on a council which he hoped would be a new Pentecost, an opening of windows for the church. It has probably been fair to say that he did not have a very clear idea of what his council would do. It was only after his death in 1963 that his successor, Pope Paul VI clarified the council's aims: It would:

- produce a document on the church;
- work for renewal of the church;
- work for the restoration of Christian unity;
- engage in dialogue with the world.

We shall see that in this programme the question of laity came up under two aspects:
- a document on the church demanded a renewed understand-

ing of the laity in the church (leading to the Constitution on the Church, *Lumen gentium*, chapter four).

- a renewal of the church demanded renewal of the laity (leading to the decree on laity *Apostolicam actuositatem*).

Vatican II was to make a remarkable change in the church's understanding of who a lay person is, despite the fact that only a few lay people had been invited as observers. Though small in numbers these made some significant contributions during the council, mainly behind the scenes. The council tried hard to do away with the pyramidal image of the church, with the Pope, bishops and clergy at the top of the pyramid and the laity at the bottom. It sought a return to the sense of the early church as a community. It did much to develop the concept of the people of God and promoted a positive definition of what it means to be a Christian The notion of Christian faithful highlighted the fact that all the members of the church share in the one baptism, the same faith, the same grace and the same vocation. All are called to holiness and the perfection of charity. Though we can find teaching and implications for the laity in all of its documents, three are particularly important for our theme.

The Constitution on the Church (Lumen gentium)

The Constitution on the Church is the most important document of the council. It seeks to give a comprehensive statement on the origins, reality and call of the church. An important feature of the document is its placing the chapter on 'The People of God' before the chapter on the hierarchy. Further, it devoted significant attention to the notion of the faithful, that is all members of the church, clerical and lay.

All the faithful of Christ of whatever rank or status are called to the fullness of the Christian life and to the perfection of charity.[3]

All are called to holiness:

All of Christ's followers, therefore, are invited and bound to pursue holiness and the perfect fulfillment of their proper state.[4]

The basic equality of the People of God is rooted in baptism.

They are incorporated into Christ through baptism. Laity and clergy both in their own special way participate in the one priesthood of Christ.

> Though they differ from one and another in essence and not only in degree, the common priesthood of the faithful and the ministerial or hierarchical priesthood are nonetheless interrelated. Each of them in its own special way is a participation in the one priesthood of Christ.[5]

The difference is based on the sacrament of ordination and the priestly character it confers. This does not take away the distinctiveness of each but stresses the relationship between them and their need of each other. In its fourth chapter, on the laity, the constitution has a very important text for the discussion of the laity in the Vatican II documents. It states:

> the term laity is here understood to mean all the faithful except those in holy orders and those who belong to a religious state approved by the church: all the faithful, that is, who by baptism are incorporated into Christ, are constituted the people of God, who have been made sharers in their own way in the priestly, prophetic and kingly office of Christ and play their part in carrying out the mission of the whole Christian people in the church and in the world.[6]

The laity are here seen positively in terms of their baptism and their active role in the people of God and negatively as non-ordained and non-religious. Baptism leads to the fundamental equality and dignity of all the Christian faithful and to their common responsibility in carrying out the mission of the church.

We can note that in Vatican II and church documents there are theologically two states: hierarchy (bishops, priests, deacons) and laity. There are, however, three canonical states, hierarchy, laity and religious. Religious who are priests belong to the theological state of hierarchy; others, the majority, who are religious brothers and sisters, belong to the theological state of laity.

This article (*LG* 31) emphasises the secular dimension as a characteristic of the laity. The distinctive feature of the laity's participation in the church's mission is that they carry out this mission precisely by being involved in family and social life and in secular activities. It is in the ordinary circumstances of their lives as homemakers, teachers, shop assistants, office workers, farmers, politicians, unemployed, retired, sick, that the laity are called to minister. This is how God calls them to sanctify the world and to bear witness to Christ. They do this by the witness of a Christian life lived in accordance with the spirit of the gospel.

This idea is further developed in *Lumen gentium* 33. The apostolate of the laity is a sharing in the saving mission of the church itself. The laity are now sharing in the mission of the church in their own right. The basis of the lay apostolate flows from the sacramental character of baptism and confirmation and is nourished by the Eucharist. However, this is the basis for all Christian apostolate and not just the laity. The laity's secular quality gives them a special vocation to bring the saving message of Jesus Christ to 'those places and circumstances where it is only through them it can become the salt of the earth'.[7] The laity can also be called to share more directly in the apostolate of the hierarchy and they can be appointed by the hierarchy to some ecclesiastical offices.

A further development in this chapter four of the Constitution on the Church is the sharing of the laity in the priestly, prophetic and kingly office of Christ (*LG* 34-36). The priestly office relates to worship in prayer and life; the prophetic office involves speaking for God in the church and the world and operating through charism; the kingly office has the aim of overcoming sin and bringing all under the Lordship of Jesus. This theme will be taken up in other conciliar and post-conciliar documents and in The Code of Canon Law.

There are two other council documents which contribute significantly to the understanding of the laity in the church, the Pastoral Constitution on the Church in the Modern World (*Gaudium et spes*) and the decree on the laity (*Apostolicam actuositatem*).

Constitution on the Church in the Modern World (Gaudium et spes)
Some of the themes referred to above are also expressed in the Pastoral Constitution on the Church in the Modern World:

Men and women were created in God's image and were commanded to conquer the earth with all it contains and to rule the world in justice and holiness: they were to acknowledge God as maker of all things and refer themselves and the totality of creation to him, so that with all things subject to God, the divine name would be glorified through all the earth.[8]

The secular nature of the laity's vocation is spelled out more specifically in *Gaudium et spes* 43:

It is their task (i.e. the laity) to cultivate a proper informed conscience and to impress the divine law on the affairs of the earthly city. For guidance and spiritual strength let them turn to the clergy; but let them realise that their pastors will not always be so expert as to have a ready answer to every problem, even every grave problem, that arises; this is not the role of the clergy: it is rather the task of lay people to shoulder their responsibilities under the guidance of Christian wisdom and with careful attention to the teaching authority of the church.[9]

Laity are, then, to be at the front in the commitment to serve the world. Their clergy may be a guide but the deepest wisdom on many issues will be found in the laity at the coalface, rather than in the clergy at the altar.

Decree on the Apostolate of the Laity (Apostolicam actuositatem)
The Decree on the Apostolate of the Laity, *Apostolicam actuositatem*, draws out further the teaching of the Constitution on the Church on the apostolate of the laity. It sees the apostolate of the laity as a sharing in the mission of the church. It focuses again on how the laity share in the priestly, prophetic and kingly office of Christ (*AA* 2). Through baptism the laity are commissioned to sanctify in Christ the priest by uniting all the activities of life to the Eucharist, thereby consecrating the world to God. They are to teach in Christ the prophet by giving witness to Christ; by exercise of the *sensus fidelium*, and by the reception and exercise of charisms. They rule or reign in Christ the king by bringing the secular world to the centre of the church and the church to the centre of the world. Christ's work of redemption, while it primarily concerns the salvation of people, also embraces the

whole temporal order. Hence the mission of the church is not only to bring the good news of Christ and his grace to men and women, but also to permeate the whole order of temporal things with the spirit of the gospel and so perfect it. The laity are called to exercise their apostolate in the church and in the world.

> The characteristic of the lay state being a life led in the midst of the world and of secular affairs, lay people are called by God to make of their apostolate ... a leaven in the world.[10]

The laity's right and duty to share in the mission of the church comes from their sharing in the Mystical Body of Christ through the sacraments of baptism and confirmation, not from the hierarchy. In a later chapter we consider charism, the special grace given by the Holy Spirit to the faithful of every rank (see *LG* 50).

In the documents of Vatican II there are enormous developments in the theology of the laity and their mission in the church. But they remain somewhat theoretical. Though as we shall see Vatican II provides a sound foundation for a spirituality of the laity, it does not articulate it. We recall the universal call to holiness as one of the remarkable statements of the council. However, how this call was to be incarnated was left unfinished. Four remarkable documents from the Holy See developed still more clearly the call to holiness and the spirituality more proper to the lay state. In addition, there would be a new breath of the Holy Spirit which would give rise to the notion of lay associate membership of a religious institute.

Achievements of the Council
Vatican II marked the beginning of a renewal movement which is still in progress. Immediately after the council there were documents, directories and instructions applying the council in many areas of church life. We could classify three major blocks of literature which arose as a direct result. Firstly, there were the documents concerned with the renewal of the liturgy, which are still emerging. Secondly, there was the revision of church law for both Latin and Eastern churches. The renewal of canon law was described by Pope John Paul II as the last document of Vatican II. However, we can point to a third block of documents which stemmed from the council and were its implementations,

namely important papal encyclicals and post-synodal exhortations: Two of these, *Christifideles laici* (The vocation and the mission of the lay faithful in the church and world, 1987) and *Vita consecrata* (Consecrated life, 1996) along with relevant sections of *The Catechism of the Catholic Church* (1994), are of particular importance for our purposes.

Code of Canon Law (1983)

As Vatican II developed it became clear that the 1917 Code of Canon Law was no longer an apt instrument for renewal of the church in a changing society. During the council, revision of the code was decreed. This revision, published in 1983, has several new points about both the Christian faith and the laity. A fundamental novelty in church law was the concept of rights and accompanying duties of the Christian faithful. The text recognised too a radical equality of all the faithful.

The Code does not actually define who the laity are; it rather determines simple personhood in the church, thus Canon 96:

> By baptism one is incorporated into the church of Christ and is constituted a person in it with duties and rights which are proper to Christians, in keeping with their condition, to the extent that they are in ecclesiastical communion and unless a legitmately issued sanction stands in the way.

The sacrament of baptism is what constitutes identity in the church. A later canon establishes that a baptised person has duties and rights which are proper to Christians and flow from baptism.

> The Christian faithful are those who, in as much as they have been incorporated in Christ through baptism, have been constituted as the people of God; for this reason, since they have become sharers in Christ's priestly, prophetic and royal office in their own manner, they are called to exercise the mission which God has entrusted to the church to fulfill in the world, in accord with the condition proper to each other.[11]

Canon 207 draws on this notion of the Christian faithful (*Christifideles*). The Christian faithful are those who have been called by baptism into the People of God. They share in their own way in the priestly, prophetic and kingly offices of Christ.

However, all groups within the *christifideles* do not have the same function. For example, the sacrament of matrimony establishes a condition and function different from holy orders or the profession of the evangelical counsels by religious. An important part of the Code is a detailed list of rights and duties for various groups in the church. Canons 208-223 state the rights and duties of all the Christian faithful, clergy and laity; Canons 224-231 state specifically the rights and duties of the lay faithful. Our special interest will be on those canons which might be seen to underscore or support lay spirituality, e.g. liturgical life, the Word of God, spiritual formation, pastoral care.

Examining these obligations and rights we see that Canon 208 stresses the equality of all the faithful flowing from baptism and the fundamental basis for the sharing of all in the mission of the church. The next canon states the duty of communion with the church and of obligations towards a particular church. Canon 210 may be seen as a basis for all spirituality:

> All Christ's faithful, each according to his or her own condition, must make a wholehearted effort to lead a holy life, and to promote the growth of the church and its continual sanctification.

It might be said to synthesise the call to holiness of Vatican II. Canon 211 lays down the obligation of mission in the church, echoing the teaching of Vatican II. Canon 212 on the church's pastors states a subsidiary right of the Christian faithful to make known their spiritual needs and communicate their vision to the pastors of the church. Canons 213-214 specifically speak about the riches of the church, and especially note the Word of God, sacraments and spirituality. Canon 215 gives the basic right of association, again based on Vatican II:

> Christ's faithful may freely establish and direct associations which serve charitable or pious purposes or which foster the Christian vocation in the world, and they may hold meetings to pursue these purposes by common effort.

Canon 217 states the right to Christian education. The final obligation of concern to us is found in canon 223 #1 which indicates that the faithful in their associations are to take account of the common good of the church, rights of others and duties to others. From this survey of the rights and duties of all members of the church it will later be clear that there is a call to holiness and some specifics about spirituality. The basis for association also lies in these canons. We shall see these all emerging in a later chapter as we consider more closely Associate Membership of a religious congregation.

Of particular interest to us, from the canons on the rights and duties of the laity, are canons 225 #1 and 225 #2. These state the rights and duties of the laity in their participation in the mission of the church and affirm their right and duty to mission in the church and the world, flowing from the sacramental character of baptism and confirmation. It is not a privilege or mandate given to them by the hierarchy. These canons restate the second Vatican Council's teaching on the secular condition of the laity. The laity are bound by a special duty to bring the good news of the kingdom to secular activities in the temporal order. They give witness to Christ and the church precisely by being engaged in secular duties. Secularity is the fundamental aspect of the mission of the laity and because of it, their everyday activities in the world take on a redemptive value. We shall note, too, the insistence on the need for sound formation in doctrinal and spiritual matters, as well as a heightening of the laity's awareness of their mission.

The authors of the 1983 Code of Canon Law tried hard to avoid a negative definition of the laity. In the end, the code focused on the notion of the Christian faithful, some of whom are clerics and some of whom are lay. Though in fact it did not succeed in giving a definition of the laity, the Code was innovative in its lists of duties and rights specific to the laity. The key notions of priestly, prophetic, and kingly offices are not carried successfully through in the later parts of the Code. One must consider as serious omissions in the 1983 Code of Canon Law the failure to vindicate the rights of lay persons to exercise personal charisms in accord with *Apostolicam actuositatem* 3 and the document on priests, *Presbyterorum ordinis* 9.

*The Vocation and Mission of the Laity in the Church and in the World
(Christifideles laici)*

The second important document comes from the 1987 synod of bishops. The synod of bishops was a new structure after Vatican II. It consisted of meetings attended by bishops, one or more representatives of the hierarchy from each country and some members of the Vatican curia. The meetings, which lasted for about three weeks, discussed topics selected by the pope. People are sometimes heard to speak darkly about the synods being manipulated or controlled, but in our area their work is very positive. Very soon the bishops concluded that a satisfactory document could not be produced in the short time frame of such meetings. As we have already noted it became customary for the pope to bring out an exhortation or some such document based on the discussions, documents or conclusions of a particular synod.[12] Some of the finest papal documents in recent decades are of this kind, e.g. the exhortation of Paul VI on evangelisation (*Evangelii nuntiandi*, 1975), the exhortation of John Paul II on laity (*Christifideles laici*, 1988) and on consecrated life (*Vita consecrata*, 1996).

Pope John Paul II's document, 'The Vocation and Mission of the Laity in the World' (*Christifideles laici*) is hugely significant. It followed on the 1987 Synod of Bishops. Possibly one of the most important aspects of this synod was the fact that prior to the synod many local churches throughout the world held consultations with the laity, thus providing some form of dialogue between the hierarchy and ordinary members of the laity who normally would not have been consulted or have had input .

The theme, which echoes throughout *Christifideles laici* is that the world is the place in which the laity are called to work and witness to the kingdom of God. The mission of the church and all its members is seen in the light of this. The call is not an option but all must work in this vineyard of the Lord.

> A new state of affairs today both in the church and in social, economic, political and cultural life, calls with a particular urgency for the action of the lay faithful ...
> Since the work that awaits everyone in the vineyard of the Lord is so great there is no place for idleness.

> With even greater urgency the 'householder' repeats his invitation: 'You go into my vineyard too.'[13]

The Pope warns against two temptations into which the laity can fall. One is the temptation to divorce faith from action, that is, separating the things of God from everyday life. This would be a return to the pre-Vatican II idea where people said their prayers and then got on with the rest of their lives. The second is the temptation to get so involved in church affairs that they neglect their primary role in secular society. Central to the vocation and mission of the laity is their secular state. It is by living out their baptismal consecration and lay vocation in the world that lay people become holy and fulfill their mission.

The world is where they receive their call from God. They live in the ordinary circumstances of family and social life, and are to see the world not as 'an external framework' but as 'the place and the means' for them to fulfil their vocation, including their priesthood.[14] Through baptism the laity are called to live a Christian vocation for the world. They are called to contribute to the sanctification of the world, 'as from within like leaven, by fulfilling their own particular duties'. Their spiritual and secular life go hand in hand. They continually bring the values of Jesus to the world thus making the world holy. They are called to work tirelessly in areas of justice, education, social affairs and economy so that all people can be set free and the kingdom of God can be proclaimed on earth. This secular quality of the laity is a gift which they bring to the church. They bring the church into the centre of the world while bringing the world into the centre of the church. This can only come about if the secular dimension of the laity is affirmed and valued as a gift in the church. To ignore the secular dimension leads to a clericalisation and lay ministries taking on clerical forms.

The Consecrated Life (Vita consecrata)

Vatican II had produced a far reaching document on the renewal of religious life (*Perfectae caritatis*, 1965). This decree led to congregations rewriting their internal legislations, usually called 'constitutions', in the light of the council. These constitutions had to be revised again after the updating of the Code of Canon Law (1983).

We now have the background needed to present and evaluate the new development in lay spirituality, which is associate membership of religious congregations.

In 1993 the synod of bishops studied the wider issue of consecrated life in the context of the decline of religious vocations in some places, and a growth of vocations in others.

In the subsequent apostolic exhortation on consecrated life (*Vita consecrata*, 1996), promulgated by John Paul II, we find some very important developments for lay spirituality which we will consider in the following chapter on associations. We will also need to consider the major document of John Paul II, *Novo millennio ineunte*, (2001) in which he welcomed the new millennium.

FURTHER READING

Church Documents

Flannery, *Vatican Two: Constitutions, Decrees,* Revised Translation in Inclusive Language (Dublin: Dominican Publications, 1996). Decree on the Apostolate of Lay People, *Apostolicam actuositatem*, 1965.

John Paul II, Apostolic Exhortation, 'The Vocation and the Mission of the Lay Faithful in the Church and in the World,' *Christifideles laici*, (London: Catholic Truth Society, 1988).

Pope Pius XII, Encyclical, *Mystici Corporis*, (1943).

Books and Articles

J. Aumann, *On the Front Lines: The Lay Person in the Church After Vatican II* (New York: Alba House, 1990).

L. Doohan, 'Lay People in the Church,' *The Way* 32 (1992) 168-177.

R. A. Duston, 'Obligations and Rights of the Lay Christian Faithful', *Angelicum* 65 (1988) 412-465.

J. Newman, *What is Catholic Action?* (Dublin: M.H. Gill, 1958).

D. Le Tourneau, *What is Opus Dei?* (Cork: Mercier Press, 1987).

A. Winters, 'Who is a Lay Person?' *The Jurist* 47 (1987) 51-70.

NOTES

1. D.P. Grigassy, 'Liturgical Movement, The' in *The New Dictionary of Theology*, ed J.A. Komonchak *et al* (Collegeville: The Liturgical Press, 1987) 586-591 for a detailed summary of the Liturgical Movement.

2. *Mystici Corporis* (1943).

3. The Constitution on the Church (*LG* 40).

4. *LG* 40

5. *LG* 10

6. *LG* 31

7. *LG* 33
8. *GS* 34
9. *GS* 43
10. *AA* 2
11. *CIC* 204
12. C. O'Donnell, 'Synod of Bishops,' *Ecclesia: A Theological Encyclopedia*, (Collegeville: The Liturgical Press, 1996) 431-433.
13. *CL* 3
14. *CL* 15

CHAPTER FOUR

The Rise of Lay Associations

One of the most important recent contributions to lay spirituality is that of lay associations. There is much interest in them on the part of laity and religious. There is not, however, a clear under-standing of what a lay association is. To add to the confusion, there are myriad forms of lay association over five continents. The term lay association will be differently understood in differ-ent places. Moreover, there are groups which many people might call lay associations but which do not accept this name.

Lay associations are another manifestation of the principle enunciated by Vatican II:

> God willed to make women and men holy and to save them not as individuals without any bond between them but rather to make them into a people who might acknowledge him and serve him in holiness. (*LG* 9)

There is not only God's call to the people of God but also many other calls to bring people together in the quest for holiness. From the beginning of the church the Holy Spirit has called into being groups and movements, each with its own charism. Thus even in New Testament times there were ranks of widows (See 1 Tim 5:3-16); soon there would be also ranks of virgins. In time there were hermits and monks. In the Middle Ages there were various groups of religious institutes but also many lay groups. Already we have alluded to groups of penitents. There were also spiritual Franciscans and Beguines, in addition to third orders and confraternities. The twentieth century saw the growth of many secular institutes, the best known of these being Opus Dei. In the 1960s and 1970s Charismatic Renewal developed, a move-ment that was largely led by laity. In various places it evolved into communities. In addition there have been vibrant move-ments like the Neo-Catechumenate, Focolare and various Christian

Life communities as well as thousands of basic Christian Communities, especially vibrant in Latin America. Less studied but of growing significance is the phenomenon of lay associate membership of religious congregations.

Before looking in detail at this new reality of lay associate membership of a religious congregation, it will be helpful to trace briefly the rise of lay associations in the church, beginning with the 1917 Code of Canon Law. This is the background to associations in the 1983 Code of Canon Law and to the subsequent development of associations in the post-conciliar life and documents of the church.

Code of Canon Law (1917)

The 1917 Code dealt with associations of the faithful in Book II, the third part of which was entitled 'The Laity' (*De laicis*). It dealt with associations of the faithful in general, canons 684 to 699 and in particular canons 700 to 725. Here two kinds of associations were distinguished: erected associations, that is ones established by church authority; and approved associations which could have developed by private initiative but whose existence was recognised by the ecclesial authority.[1]

Three levels of authority had the power to erect or recognise associations: the pope, the diocesan bishops, and those who have been given this power by papal privilege. Various associations were recognised. These corresponded with the ends for association specified by canon 685 which included pursuing spiritual perfection, fostering works of piety or charity and promoting worship.

The 1917 Code recognised three kinds of associations:[2]

1. Secular third orders which indicated their lay character and their membership or affiliation to religious orders, mostly pre-Reformation. These secular third orders promoted the Christian perfection of their members according to the spirituality of the parent order.

2. Confraternities, whose purpose was the promotion of public worship and piety, e.g. the confraternities of the Sacred Heart, the Blessed Sacrament, the Brown Scapular, the Rosary etc.

3. Pious Unions, whose purpose was works of charity or piety.

Associate membership of a religious congregation, the association which will be looked at in detail later in this chapter, does not really fit into the norms or structures of the 1917 Code. In aims it is closest to secular third orders but in structures it is perhaps closest to pious unions. Associate membership resembles the secular third orders in that the associate members seek to grow in holiness through living the charism of the institute in their daily lives in the world. It also resembles the third order somewhat in its liturgical and prayer life. The third order differs from associate membership in that the third order has a Rule, noviceship, profession and in some places a habit. The first order also has some authority for the internal government and the spiritual development of the members, and therefore the third order more truly resembles the tight structure of religious life than the flexible associate membership of today.

The associate membership that we are considering resembles more the 1917 Code's description of pious unions. The approval of the Ordinary, that is, the local bishop, is sufficient for the establishment of a pious union. A pious union strives to cultivate among its members a life of piety, along with corporal or spiritual works of mercy. It is therefore clear that we are dealing with a new reality with the birth of lay association. It would be helpful at this stage to note carefully the difference between first, second, and third orders.

First, Second and Third Orders

In the ancient or medieval orders the 'First order' was that of men religious, not necessarily ordained, pursuing the evangelical counsels under vow in community according to their rule. The 'second order' was of women religious pursuing the same goals, following a similar rule and usually under the spiritual guidance of a member of the 'first order'.

In the twelfth and thirteenth centuries, many lay people associated themselves with either congregation, sometimes living with them and pursuing the spirit of the community but without vows and still involved in the 'world'. These were called 'third orders'. These 'third orders' were recognised by St Francis of Assisi who gave the Francisian third order a rule, approved by Pope Honorius I in 1221. In 1285 the Dominican Order received a similar rule which was sanctioned in 1406. Later the Augustinians, Servites, the Carmelites, the Minims, the Trinitarians and the Norbertines had rules approved. In time there would be vows in third orders. These vows were to live the evangelical counsels according to one's state in life. Nowadays we can find third order vows sometimes replaced by promises or other commitments.

There is a further complication. Some orders have a second order of enclosed, contemplative nuns, e.g. Carmelites, Dominicans, Franciscans. But there are also active sisters living in community like modern religious, such as the Sisters of St Clare, Dominicans Sisters, various Carmelite Sisters. These are called 'third order regular'. They are religious living with vows in community. Secular third orders do not live in community and do not have vows.

The Secular Institute

Another category of life in the church is that of secular institutes. A secular institute is a group whose members lead a consecrated life in the world: they strive for the perfection of charity and work for the evangelisation of the world in their everyday life. They are called to be a 'leaven' in the world (see Luke 13:20-21). Outwardly, for example in their activities, associations and secular institutes may seem similar. There is, however, a key difference lying in the fact that secular institutes are canonically regarded as forms of consecrated life which is seen as a strengthening of the baptismal commitment. These institutes differ from religious life in that the evangelical counsels are lived in the world, in prayer and work and ordinary life. They can be seen also as leaven within the laity.

Developments

After the promulgation of the 1917 Code many ecclesiastical associations were erected. Lay associations were often founded on the initiative of persons other than church authorities. A very noteworthy one of these was the Legion of Mary (1921) founded in Ireland by a layman, Frank Duff.

Three other events influenced the development of associations of the faithful between the 1917 Code and the beginning of Vatican II. Firstly, the Society of St Vincent de Paul, though commended and recognised by church authorities, never looked for formal ecclesiastical approval. It remained a lay society. This would eventually have a large influence on the history of associations. In November 1920, the lay status of the St Vincent de Paul Society was reaffirmed by the Vatican in a decree which also stated that the society was not subject to the local bishop in the same way as those ecclesiastical societies covered in canons 686-699. This decree reclaimed the right of the Christian faithful to form associations without the intervention of the hierarchy.

Secondly, associations developed as a result of the call to the church of Pope Pius XI to support Catholic Action. As has been seen earlier, Catholic Action was apostolic activity carried out by the laity under the mandate of the hierarchy. Through his encouragement Catholic Action spread around the world. It aimed to bring Christian witness to society through a spirituality that related to a life lived in the world.

In 1957 Pope Pius XII defined Catholic Action as a 'co-operation in the apostolate of the hierarchy'. He also redefined Catholic Action to include all groups through which lay people exercised an apostolate, thus broadening the concept and it now included many groups which did not neatly fit into the mould of the three categories mentioned in the 1917 Code, i.e. secular third orders, pious unions and confraternities.

Thirdly, a noteworthy canonist of the time, Mattheo Conte A. Coronata saw that there was a problem in distinguishing approved societies from those commended by ecclesiastical authority.[3] He felt that there was need for a fourth kind of association of the faithful. In 1945 the Sacred Congregation for Religious appointed a commission of five canonists to consider this question and make recommendations. Their findings resulted in the creation of a new canonical body, namely the secular institute. Quite a number of the pious unions founded between 1790 and 1947 adopted this novel canonical status.

Vatican II

As a result of this confusion about associations there was need for reform and clarity. Associations became a topic for discussion on the Vatican II agenda (1962-1965). The Preparatory

Commission for the Discipline of the Clergy and the Laity looked at the whole question. The Commission repeated some of the 1917 Code of Canon Law but also suggested changes for lay and ecclesiastical associations. It recognised the right of the faithful to found associations on their own initiative; these groups were to be called 'private' rather than 'lay'. These proposals were never voted on. They were sent to the pontifical commission engaged in revising the Code of Canon Law .

The main teaching of Vatican II on associations of the faithful can be found in the Decree on the Apostolate of Lay People, (*Apostolicam actuositatem*). Vatican II stated a preference for those associations which fostered spiritual growth within the context of every day life and met the needs of the times.

There is a great variety of apostolic association. Some serve the general apostolic purposes of the church; others aim specifically at evangelisation and sanctification; others work for the permeation of the temporal order by the Christian spirit; and others engage in works of mercy and of charity as their special way of bearing witness to Christ. First among these associations to be given consideration should be those which favour and promote a more intimate unity between the faith of the members and their everyday life. Associations are not ends in themselves; they are meant to be of service to the church's mission to the world.[4]

The decree affirmed the right of the laity to found and run associations on their own initiative. This was a major breakthrough in that it recognised the laity's own role in the mission of the church as a right; associations were no longer a means by which the laity shared in the hierarchy's mission. Based on their baptismal dignity all the Christian faithful share a common concern for building up the body of Christ (*LG* 32). This equality through baptism provided a new basis for addressing fundamental rights in the church and for the 1983 Canon Law reform.

Code of Canon Law (1983)

For our purposes there are two places in the 1983 Code of Canon Law which deal with associations. The first is included in the rights and duties of all the members of the church who are seen as having a right to assembly for charitable or pious purposes.

> Christ's faithful may freely establish direct associations
> which serve charitable or pious purposes or which foster the
> Christian vocation in the world, and they may hold meetings
> to pursue these purposes by common effort.[5]

This canon can be seen to reflect contemporary international law
on human rights, which include the right to assemble for aims
that are religious, political, cultural etc. Canon 215 covers a variety of situations in which people might come together in the
church, once-off groupings for a particular need, more stable
groupings for charitable purposes, or for prayer, study, self help
etc. On the basis of this fundamental right there are now many
forms of association recognised by law at parish, diocesan, and
universal levels: these serve ways of living the gospel, they provide liturgical life, they serve various needs, they can be consult-
ative bodies in the church.

The other main canons on associations are canons 298-329.
They are under the following headings: 1) Common Norms; 2)
On Public Associations of the Christian Faithful; 3) Private
Associations of the Christian Faithful; 4) Special Norms on
Associations of the Faithful.

The common norms name several different kinds of association:

> In the church there are associations distinct from institutes of
> consecrated life and societies of apostolic life, in which the
> Christian faithful, either clergy or laity, or clergy and laity to-
> gether, strive by common effort to promote a more perfect
> life or to foster public worship or Christian doctrine or to ex-
> ercise other apostolic works, namely to engage in efforts of
> evangelisation, and to animate the temporal order with a
> Christian spirit.[6]

The main characteristic of these associations of the faithful is
that, unlike institutes of consecrated life, they have no vows. The
faithful have the right to set up private associations; some might
seek recognition by the competent authority. Associations are
called public when set up by the church itself. Canon 303 recog-
nises third orders and similar associations.

Associations whose members lead an apostolic life and strive
for Christian perfection while living in the world and who

share the spirit of some religious institute under the higher direction of that same institute are called third orders or some other appropriate name.[7]

Third orders alone are explicitly treated elsewhere in Canon Law.

There are some further points of interest in the 1983 Code. Canon 304 states that all associations of the faithful, whether public or private, must have their own statutes. These are to state the association's aims and objectives, how it is governed, the conditions for membership, who draws up its policies according to culture and times.

Canon 307 #3 allows members of institutes of consecrated life, with the approval of their superior, to join associations of the faithful even though these associations are lay. Associations must be outward looking. Canon 311 states that members of the institutes of consecrated life who are responsible for third orders or for associations linked with the spirit of the institute are to make sure that the associations are involved in the apostolate of the diocese.

In its section on Public Associations of the Christian Faithful, (Canons 249-253) the Code lays down the authorities competent to erect public associations. Another canon 312 #2 is very important for associations such as third orders or associations which reflect the spirit of the institute.

The consent given by a diocesan bishop for the erection of a house of a religious institute also allows for the erection in the same house of an association proper to the institute.

What is stated here is the right of any religious community, independently of the bishop, to erect associations. One could see that this norm of the Code might open the way to such associations being a normal or regular feature of religious houses.

The Code's 'Special Norms for Associations of the Laity' begins by stating that lay members of the Christian faithful 'are to esteem greatly associations established for spiritual purposes' which 'strive by common effort to promote a more perfect life'. It also contains two directives for those who preside over associations of the laity. They are to see that their association co-operates with other associations in their territory and provides their members with apostolic formation. Elsewhere in the Code, Canon 677 states:

> Institutes, which have associations of Christ's faithful joined to them, are to have a special care that these associations are imbued with the genuine spirit of their religious family.

We shall see later that the vitality of associate membership of a religious congregation depends largely on formation and on healthy relationships with the religious institute.

During the 1980s, and especially after the promulgation of the 1983 Code of Canon Law, the Pontifical Council for the Laity held a series of international meetings which led to a further understanding and development of associations in the church. From the Code therefore we have encouragement and legislation for associations of various kinds. There are also a few but very significant canons which address lay associate membership of a religious institutes.

The Vocation of the Laity in the Church and World (Christifideles laici)

We have several times referred to the important document on the laity, *Christifideles laici*. By the time of its writing associations had developed. In chapter two the pope stated how in recent years the church has experienced a great growth in the spread of new forms of associations. Many different terms were used to describe these associations, from small Christian communities, ecclesial communities, base communities, secular institutes, third orders, groups and movements. Generally these associations were welcomed by the Synod of Bishops, with bishops seeing them as invaluable for the church, as constituting a true enrichment of its evangelistic works, as a sign of hope, a sign of the activity of the Spirit, as a new way of being church today and a gift to the church. The Synod of Bishops saw them as positive in helping the laity to grow in holiness and live their baptismal consecration with greater fervour.

Bishop Paul Cordes, Vice-President of the Pontifical Council of the Laity, spoke of the need for bishops to be open to receiving the new charisms being given by the Spirit to the new movements and associations in the church, stating that the church's pastors are not masters of the charisms, but rather servants of 'the same spirit that animates the movements'.

Pope John Paul, in *Christifideles laici*, reaffirmed this positive approach to lay associations and movements (nn 29-31). He stated that the period after Vatican II was a new season of associations in the church and a sign of the Spirit who continues to inspire new aspirations towards holiness and the participation of so many lay faithful in the flourishing of groups, associations and spiritual movements.[8]

Even though these associations can be very different from each other in structure or form, they have a common purpose to participate in the mission of the church and to be a source of hope and witness to the gospel. These associations must be a 'sign of communion' in themselves and for the whole church community.[9]

There is an ecclesial right to form associations. John Paul goes on to restate what had been previous stated in the documents of Vatican II and in the 1983 Code of Canon Law, that the rights of lay people to form associate groups comes from their baptism, which calls the lay faithful to participate in the life and mission of the church. It is not derived from any kind of mandate from the bishops.[10]

The exhortation, in article 30, lists five criteria for the discernment of the authenticity of lay associations.[11]

- The primacy given to the call of every Christian to holiness.
- The responsibility of professing the Catholic faith.
- The witness to a strong and authentic communion with the pope and the local bishop and esteem for all forms of the church's apostolate.
- Conformity to, and participation in, the church's apostolic goals, i.e. the evangelisation and sanctification of humanity and the Christian formation of people's conscience.
- A commitment to a presence in human society.

John Paul II warns of the dangers of associations becoming 'parallel' churches or of ignoring pastoral teaching or the building up of the church community. Each association should be filled with a missionary zeal and a hunger for a more loving and just society. It is important to note that many of the interventions of the Synod of Bishops on lay associations saw the greatest reason for forming associations as a desire on the part of the laity to respond to the universal call to holiness and to develop a lay spirituality.

The papal document, in article 30 also, gives a list of the fruits which associations, following the above criteria, have produced:

- A renewed appreciation of prayer, contemplation, liturgical and sacramental life.
- A reawakening of vocations to Christian marriage, priesthood and religious life.
- A readiness to participate in programmes and church activities at local, national and international level.
- A commitment to be a Christian witness in the various situations of social life.
- A commitment to catechesis and Christian formation.
- A spirit of detachment and evangelical poverty leading to greater sharing with the poor.
- Conversion to the Christian Life or the return to church of those members who had fallen away.

The discernment of associations by the pope, and his hopes for them, mark a new stage in the development of lay spirituality.

Apostolic Exhortation on Consecrated Life (Vita consecrata)
The exhortation on the laity spoke positively but in a general way about lay associations. The specific form of associate membership with religious institutes, which is the topic of this study, is treated in yet another post synodal exhortation on consecrated life (*Vita consecrata*) which Pope John Paul II promulgated in 1996. It was addressed to the bishops and clergy, religious orders and congregations, societies of apostolic life, secular institutes and all the faithful.

In the second chapter (*Signum fraternitatis*) he notes how lay people recognise the value of consecrated life. They seek to attach themselves to religious congregations, sharing their spirituality and/or assisting in their apostolates. These associations should be fostered and formed so that the laity appreciate their lay vocation more deeply and give themselves to the apostolate.[12] Article 56 of the apostolic exhortation mentions the increasing number of associates and lay volunteers joined to institutes of consecrated life. This he asserts should be held in great esteem. The pope encourages a proper formation of these associates so that they approach their apostolate with 'supernaturally motivated intentions and a strong sense of community'. Lay persons in decision-making positions in these associations should promote the ends of the institute and be accountable to the 'competent superiors'. There is an need for special directives in each institute, which should indicate the responsibilities of the institute, its communities and associate members. Association should always be careful to protect the identity of the institute.

This exhortation despite its theme, consecrated life, is extremely important for the development of lay associate membership of religious congregations. We have already noted the few canons in the1983 Code which foresee the possibility of such associations and give general norms. Writing in 1996 the pope specifically encourages this new form of life and indicates the importance of bonds with a religious institute.Though short, this passage provides a springboard for all kinds of further development. Two years later, at the World Congress of Ecclesial Movements and New Communities, associate members of some religious congregations were present.

There are several reasons for the growth of lay associates with religious institutes. Firstly, there was a fresh interest in spirituality. Secondly, religious institutes after Vatican II had been told to look at their heritage and charism. Many religious discovered important elements of lay involvement, affiliation or association at an earlier period of their existence. These bonds were very often not structured but were nevertheless significant. Thirdly, a decline in numbers in many religious institutes spurred them on to share their charism more widely. At an earlier time such sharing would have been to attract vocations. Now religious discovered that people were drawn to the charism but were not prepared or able to become members of the institute by religious profession. Religious were naturally anxious that their charism should not die. They saw a place for their heritage in the secular world. Lay people could give new expressions to their charisms. Moreover, lay people were beginning to be drawn by the spirituality of religious congregations. It is in this climate of a fresh appreciation and presentation of their charism by reli-gious, along with the developing interest of laity in spirituality, that we find a *kairos*, or sacred opportunity, for the birth of new forms of lay spirituality.

Providentially, there had been sufficient associations in exis-tence for canon law to have taken account of them. There was then a quite specific coming together of laity who were associated with a religious congregation. There are three levels in the assoc-iation of religious and laity:

- sharing of the spiritual life;
- common life under the same roof;
- association for a definite mission.

Lay associate membership can be seen as yet another manifest-ation of the gift of the Holy Spirit helping the church to read 'the signs of the times'. The Constitution on the Church in the Modern World asserts that God is at work in human history and the church must respond.

> It is for God's people as a whole, with the help of the Holy Spirit, and especially pastors and theologians, to listen to the various voices of our day, discerning them, and interpreting them, and to evaluate them in the light of the Word of God.[13]

Since one of the 'signs of the times' is surely the hunger for spiri-tuality, together with a new clarity about the identity and her-itage of religious congregations, it is therefore the right moment for the development of lay associate membership of religious congregations.

Before Vatican II and the subsequent Code of Canon Law, only what were canonically 'religious orders' (almost all pre-Reformation) could have secular third orders attached to them. Today many religious congregations have members of the laity associated with them, sharing their spirituality, charism and joining in their apostolate. Others are looking at the possibility of having some form of associate membership. Law and practice are still evolving.

Associate membership is a manifestation of the Holy Spirit present in the church today. It is the desire of a considerable number of lay men and women, single and married, who wish to share, to collaborate in the charism, spirituality and mission of religious institutes through some form of association. It is also seen as a response of many religious institutes to a new openness to the laity and a willingness to share their charisms, spirituality and mission with them. It is a new way in which the Holy Spirit is working in religious life, to keep alive the spirit and founding charism of religious congregations, where numbers are declining. It is a response to a need within the church today, to help the laity take a fuller role in the life and mission of the church. Through associate membership, religious contribute to the building of the church by sharing with and forming the laity in spirituality, and by training them to take their rightful place in the mission of the church. Christopher O'Donnell, speaking about religious life, stated that:

> when charism is linked with apostolate, through sharing it with others, new life is infused into the congregations and the charism will be found to have a wider application than was suspected and the church itself will be enabled to share more deeply in it.[14]

Thus with the renewal of religious life after Vatican II many congregations looked at the possibility of closer links and collaboration with the laity. The laity, in their turn, having become more aware of their call to holiness and the perfection of charity, looked to the religious for guidance and support. This eventually gave rise to the development of lay associate membership of a religious congregation as we know it today. We should note that men or women are members of both male and female congregations. Many names are used to describe lay associate membership:

- Co-Members
- Partners
- Associate Members
- Co-Workers
- Shared Membership
- Affiliated Members
- Auxiliary Members
- Prayer Associates
- Companions
- Voluntary Helpers

- Oblates
- Extended Membership

In each of the above, the relationship between the parent congregation and the lay members varies greatly. It can range at one end of the scale from living in community for one or two years with the religious and working alongside them, sometimes taking vows, to at the other end of the scale, a very loose connection, little contact by the lay members other than praying for the congregation and maybe friendship with some of the religious.

In the next chapter we will look at associate membership of religious congregations in a more developed form. This involves some process of selection, a sharing of charism, spirituality, some sense of community/family spirit between the religious and laity, a sense of sharing in mission and finally a formation programme leading to some form of commitment.

By looking at the more developed form, we can see some of the possibilities of this new phenomenon as well as difficulties and problematic areas. Such an exploration should be of value even to congregations and laity whose associate membership is less structured or evolved.

FURTHER READING

Church Documents

T. L. Bouscaren, *Canon Law: A Text and Commentary* (Milwaukee: The Bruce Publishing Co, 1939) in canons 87, 107, 948 at 355-358.

E. Kneal, 'Associations of the Christian Faithful,' in *The Code of Canon Law: A Text and Commentary*, eds J. Coriden *et al* (New York/ Mahwah: Paulist Press, 1985) at 244-257.

John Paul II, Apostolic Exhortation, 'The Consecrated Life and its Mission in the Church and in the World,' *Vita consecrata* (London: Catholic Truth Society, 1996).

Articles

J. Amos, 'A Legal History of Associations of the Faithful,' *Studia canonica* 21 (1987) 271-297.

R. Goldie, 'A Roman Window on the Lay Movements,' *Priests & People* 13 (1999) 45-49.

F. G. Morrisey, 'The Laity in the New Code of Canon Law,' *Studia canonica* 1 (1983) 135-148.

F. R. Mc Manus, 'The Laity in Church Law, New Code, New Focus,' *The Jurist* (1987) 11-31.

A. Prew-Winters, 'Who is a Lay Person?' *The Jurist* 47 (1987) 51-70.

NOTES

1. T. L. Bouscaren, *Canon Law: A Text and Commentary* (Milwaukee: The Bruce Publishing Co, 1939) canons 87, 107, 948 at 355-358
2. Code of Canon Law (1917) 700, 702, 707
3. See A. Jacobs, 'Les associations des fidèles,' *Studia canonica* 22 (1988) 359-379 at 362
4. The Decree on the Apostolate of the Laity (*AA* 19)
5. The Code of Canon Law (1983) 215
6. Canon (1983) 298
7. Canon (1983) 303
8. *Christifideles laici* (*CL*) 29
9. Ibid
10. *CL* 31
11. *CL* 30
12. The Consecrated Life, *Vita consecrata* (1996) 41-71
13. The Constitution on the Church in the Modern World, *GS* 44
14. See C. O'Donnell, 'Religious Community as Apostolic Resource', *Religious Life Review* 24 (1985) 307-313 at 313.

CHAPTER FIVE

Elements of Associate Membership
of Religious Congregations

The fruitful development of lay associate membership with religious institutes involves a difficult dialogue between religious and laity. The topic of the dialogue revolves around the heritage of the religious institute and lay spirituality. The difficulty of this dialogue arises from the lack of experience on the part of both partners of the life situation of the other. Religious know their heritage but they will not be the ones to indicate how its values are to be incarnated in the lay state. The laity, on the other hand, will have a sense of their own state. They will be very conscious of, even 'allergic' to, anything that tends to make them religious; however, they must learn from religious a living heritage which is to be adopted and adapted to the lay state.

In this dialogue, then, there is the need for both parties to imagine themselves in the shoes of the other. The laity look at the heritage that has been handed on by religious. Religious look at both their heritage and the lay state.

A problem may arise if there is a failure by religious to present the charism and heritage in a way that gives opportunities for lay spirituality to develop. Religious are often inclined to think that they know the lay state. After all, they were lay themselves before they joined religious life. Unknown to themselves they can easily impose the culture of religious life as the norm, instead of presenting their charism for lay incarnation. They have ideas about being lay but lack present experience. This issue is more difficult among religious who have sought in recent decades to play down the difference between religious and lay life. If religious have a blurred view of their authentic identity, it will be hard to communicate their own heritage in a way acceptable to lay expectations.

Perhaps the most basic difficulty arises from the failure of either or both parties in the dialogue to appreciate the newness of lay associate membership with a religious institute. Religious have to learn to see their heritage in lay clothes, while laity have to be open to a rich way of life without being too fearful that it might come with a religious habit.

As we come now to look at this new phenomenon, there is an urgency arising from the reiteration by Pope John Paul II of holiness as a pastoral problem in the new millennium. The pope stressed the teaching of Vatican II that it is not simplistic and he knew that stating the call to holiness would not be enough.

In the document which presented the challenges of the new millennium (*Novo millennio ineunte*) he stated:

> The time has come to re-propose wholeheartedly to everyone this high standard of ordinary Christian living: the whole life of the Christian community and of Christian families must lead in this direction. It is also clear, however, that the paths to holiness are personal and call for genuine 'training in holiness', adapted to people's needs. This training must integrate the resources offered to everyone with both the traditional forms of individual and group assistance, as well as the more recent forms of support offered in associations and movements recognised by the church. (n 31)

This encouragement from Pope John Paul II is significant.

Over the last number of years as Associate Co-ordinator of the Daughters of Mary and Joseph, I have been interested in associate membership also in other congregations. I have become increasing convinced that there are six key elements of associate membership of a religious congregation. These will be manifested somewhat differently in each congregation.

- Charism / gift of the Holy Spirit
- Spirituality / Prayer life
- Community / Family Spirit / Togetherness
- Mission / Ministry / Apostolate / Social Concern
- Commitment / Response
- Formation / Growth

Each Associate Group will usually work at establishing its own associate legislation, such as statutes or constitutions, directives and formation programme. We will look at each of the above in turn.

It will be seen that these six elements have been at the heart of the renewal of religious life mandated by Vatican II. They may not immediately resonate with laity in the pew but it will be seen that the six are vital for authentic lay spirituality. When we look at any religious heritage or lay spirituality we will notice that it does not differ from others in the component parts, such as scripture, sacraments, prayer, virtuous living etc, but in the emphasis given to the elements common to all genuine Christian search for holiness. A contemplative vocation will give more attention to prayer, but all need some degree of commitment to prayer. Those whose life is primarily engaged in works of mercy are not alone in this service. All are called to serve others in works of love and mercy.

In the same way, when we look at the six elements we will find that they probably apply to all examples of associate membership but with varying degrees of emphasis and interest.

CHARISM

It will be helpful to look at charism in some detail in order to appreciate the Spirit-filled reality of lay associate membership of a religious institute. The word 'charism' is frequently misunderstood. The teaching of the scripture was largely forgotten in the church for nearly 1600 years. Vatican II and later documents invited the church to look again at the New Testament and subsequent history, the better to understand the present work of the Holy Spirit in the church.

Charism in the New Testament

The word 'charism' is derived from the Greek word *charis* meaning a free gift; it is therefore used in theology for a spiritual capacity resulting from God's grace. There are four lists of charisms in the New Testament (1 Cor 1: 4-7; 1 Cor 12: 9-10, 28-31; Rom 12:4-8; Eph 4:11-13). It is generally agreed that in these a charism is understood to be a gift of the Holy Spirit bestowed upon an individual Christian for the sake of building up the community.

The basis for the presence of such gifts or charisms is the continually abiding presence of the Holy Spirit in the Christian community.[1] Indeed the charisms can be seen as the manifestation or proof of that presence. The charisms have no validity or claim to existence apart from the Spirit. In 1 Pet 4:10-11 the various gifts or charisms are divided into two classes: speaking gifts and serving gifts. Both must be used for the benefit of others and for the glory of God. It is also implied that each person has received a gift. Some gifts manifest the quiet and abiding presence of the Spirit, e.g. knowledge, wisdom, faith, generosity, mercy. They are not merely natural virtues but real gifts of grace which enable the recipients to contribute to the upbuilding of the community in their own unique way. Others manifest the power of the Spirit, e.g. prophecy, discernment, healings, preaching, leadership, service. Love is not enumerated among the gifts; it is a 'more excellent way' within which all the charisms operate (see 1 Cor 12:31). The New Testament makes it clear that the possession of charisms is no guarantee of personal holiness. Those Corinthians with charisms in 1 Cor 3:1-3, 14-17 showed that weakness and sin were present among them.

The Early Centuries

In the first three centuries of the church's life, the charisms indicated in the New Testament continued to be present and recognised. Martyrdom was seen as an important charism. Someone who gave his/her life or experienced imprisonment or torture was seen as having gifts of the Holy Spirit in a special way. From about the fourth century there was a significant change, arising largely out of fear of the use of charism by some heretical movements such as the Montanists. There was, too, a growth in episcopal power, authority and clericalisation. The Montanists were highly enthusiastic people who felt led by the Spirit and who rejected the institutional church. Charism became distrusted and was soon peripheral.

The Counter Reformation

The Protestant Reformation, followed by the Counter Reformation, led to further marginalisation of charisms as the church became increasingly suspicious of extraordinary phenomena . A view called 'Dispensationalism' was widely held. It held that while charisms had been essential in the early church, they had disappeared after the first few centuries of the church, apart from their appearance in the lives of some of the saints.

Pre-Vatican II

At the end of the nineteenth century the presence of charism in the church became an important issue in both Protestant and Catholic ecclesiology. Pope Leo XIII in his encyclical *Divinum illud* (1896) described the Holy Spirit as the 'soul of the church' and stated that charisms continued to serve the good in the church. However, in later encyclicals he spoke of the tension between the institutional church and charisms and expressed concern that overemphasis on charisms might lead to a down playing of the magisterium. Bringing about a balance between the charisms and the magisterium was a important aspect of the ecclesiological teaching of Pope Pius XII. In his encyclical on the mystical body of Christ (*Mystici corporis*, 1943) he stated that there should be no problem between charisms and the magisterium; the church was neither composed only of charismatic gifts nor only institutional ones, but these complemented each other.

Vatican II

Charism continued to be an issue at the beginning of the Second Vatican Council. In an important debate in the second session (1963) Cardinal Ruffini held the 'dispensationalist' view. The opposite position was held by Cardinal Suenens who held that charism belonged to the very essence of the church. His opinion eventually won over the council. The church now returned to the New Testament idea that the presence of charisms is a normal aspect of the church and concerns all its members. The main treatment of charism is in *LG* 12:

> It is not only through the sacraments and the ministries that the Holy Spirit makes the people holy.... Allotting his gifts 'at will to each individual' (1 Cor 12:11), he also distributes special graces among the faithful of every rank. By these gifts, he makes them fit and ready to undertake various tasks and offices for the renewal and building up of the church, as it is written, 'the manifestation of the spirit is given to everyone for profit.' (1 Cor 12:7) Whether these charisms be very remarkable or more simple and widely diffused, they are to be received with thanksgiving and consolation since they are primarily suited to and useful for the needs of the church.[2]

These graces are called 'special' because of the way in which they are given directly by the Spirit and because of their purpose which is service of the church. There are two other major texts on charism that are of special relevance to the laity. One is from the decree on the ministry and life of priests, (*Presbyterorum ordinis*):

> While testing the spirits to discover if they be of God, they (priests) must discover with faith, recognise with joy and foster diligently the many and varied charisms of the laity.[3]

Priests should be talent-scouts, seeking out the charism of the laity. Such gifts are not to be seen as threats; they contribute powerfully to the mission of the church.

The other text is from the decree on the apostolate of lay people (*Apostolicam actuositatem*):

> The Holy Spirit 'gives the faithful special gifts besides (see 1 Cor 12:7) 'allotting them to each just as the Spirit chooses'(1 Cor 12:11), so that, putting at the service of others the grace received, all may be 'good stewards of God's varied gifts,'(1 Pet 4:10) for the building up of the whole body in charity (see Eph 4:16). From the reception of these charisms, even the most ordinary ones, there follows for all Christian believers the right and duty to use them in the church and in the world for the good of humanity and the development of the church.[4]

Clearly charisms are essential to the church and should figure strongly in the life of the laity. It is hard, however, to see the laity exercising this rightful duty unless encouraged and formed within the community, especially by pastors.

Charism and Associate Membership

One of the major examples of charism within in the church is religious life. Vatican II notes that religious life is not a middle road between the clergy and laity and speaks of it in terms of its charismatic calling. The decree on religious life (*Perfectae caritatis*) also calls on religious life to return to its founding charism, to the 'primitive inspiration' of the institute.

It is to the church's advantage that each institute has its own proper character and function. Therefore the spirit and aims of each founder should be faithfully acknowledged and maintained, as indeed should each institute's sound traditions, for all of these constitute an institute's heritage.[5]

In the period since Vatican II there has been a fuller reception of religious life as charismatic. The Apostolic Exhortation on the Renewal of Religious Life (*Evangelica testificatio*, 1971), speaks both of the charisms of the founders and of the charism of religious life.[6]

Religious life is clearly charismatic. Associate membership of a religious congregation will be charismatic both in receiving and applying a religious heritage and in finding a new way of lay spirituality. As we have seen earlier, associate membership is a response to a special call to live out a particular charism as a lay person alongside vowed members of a religious congregation. Therefore associate members will be attracted by the charism of a particular congregation. For example, a congregation which has a charism of mercy and compassion will draw the associate members to these virtues and to an openness to these charisms. They may have already to some extent the seed of the charism of mercy within them. They will feel drawn to allow it grow within them. The Lord brings people to him through the circumstances of their lives (see John 12:32). It is in their own life experiences and need of the Lord's mercy and compassion that they have been strengthened, loved and given the courage to use the charism of mercy for others. The Lord brings them closer to himself through their strengths and weaknesses. Through that ongoing need of conversion, they will be freed, gifted and called to share with others that love and mercy they have received to be instruments of mercy for others. Others can be touched by seeing religious answer the cry of the poor and want somehow to share in this corner of the vineyard. Again, people can be attracted by something about a religious whom they know and admire; they then seek what makes their religious friend 'tick'. Another example might be of a person, drawn to prayer, finding through this charism an attraction towards some contemplative congregation. Others may have read an important book from a spiritual tradition, and have then been drawn to the religious institute which seems to live the values in the spiritual classic. Associates will grow in and live and radiate the charism of their parent congregation through God's gift to them, and through prayerfully reflecting and living out in their lives the spirit of the Founder as mediated to them by the congregation.

SPIRITUALITY / PRAYER LIFE

The second very important element of associate membership is spirituality/prayer life. As we have seen already, Vatican II made a radical change in the understanding of who a lay person is and proclaimed the call to holiness of all the baptised. The council and subsequent church documents stressed the importance of the secular vocation of the laity. It is important that the associates understand the term 'lay spirituality', and that this has relevance for their lives. They must take seriously the call of Vatican II to play their part in the mission of the whole people of God in the church and the world and so work to bring about the kingdom of God on earth.

Aspects of Lay Associate Spirituality
It is essential not to impose a spirituality on associates that is suitable for a convent or monastery or is a lesser version of the spirituality of religious. Therefore it is of vital importance to state that the spirituality of associate members of a religious congregation will be a spirituality adapted and suited to the everyday, secular life of the associates. They will grow in holiness, love of God and of neighbour precisely through their lay state, enriched by a spirituality already given to the church in a religious family.

In Christian life lived to the full there are several elements that one would expect to find in the Catholic tradition. They are found in all religious congregations and will feature in the spirituality of lay associate members of a religious congregation. Such are:
- The Eucharist
- Scripture / Word of God
- Liturgical Prayer
- Devotion to Mary
- Devotion to the Saints

- Personal Prayer
- Shared Prayer

We shall look briefly at each in turn. However, before doing so it is necessary again to point out that in any spirituality the order, emphasis and balance of the above aspects will vary and be highlighted according to the particular spirituality of the parent congregation, and likewise of the emerging lay spirituality of the associates. For example, a congregation which has a Marian spirituality, will mediate this charism to the associate members and it will be taken up by them and expressed in a lay mode or form that is Marian. Congregations with a strong Eucharistic devotion or devotion to a saint will reflect this orientation in its prayer and life, and the lay associates will feel drawn to live such dimensions in their secular lives

The Eucharist

The Eucharist, 'the source and summit of the Christian life' (*LG* 11), will be the centre of the associate's spirituality and associate membership The two tables of the Word and the Eucharist provide strength and spiritual nourishment and are the centre of Christian life and living. Everything the Christian does is capable of being offered along with the sacrifice of Christ.

The Eucharist is the heart of the church. Through the celebration of the Eucharist members of the Christian community are strengthened to go out on mission, to serve God's kingdom on earth. At the end of every Eucharist they are commissioned, sent to love and serve the Lord. A strong sense of the community aspect of the Eucharist is important for the spirituality of associates. Everything that they do has its truest meaning when related to the Eucharist. Vatican II notes:

The church, therefore, spares no effort in trying to ensure that, when present at the mystery of faith (the Eucharist) Christian believers should not be there as strangers or silent spectators. On the contrary, having a good grasp of it through the rites and prayers, they should take part in the sacred action, actively, fully aware and devoutly. They should be formed by God's Word, and be nourished at the table of the Lord's Body. They should give thanks to God. Offering the immaculate victim, not only through the hands of the priest but also together with him, they should learn to offer themselves. Through Christ, the Mediator, they should be drawn day by day into ever more perfect union with God and each other, so that finally God may be all in all.[7]

Scripture/Word of God

Vatican II in its Constitution on Divine Revelation, *Dei Verbum*, firmly established the central place of sacred scripture in the life of the church and encouraged all the faithful to learn the 'surpassing knowledge of Jesus Christ' (Phil 3:8) by frequent reading of the divine scriptures (*DV* 25). It goes on to quote the phrase of Saint Jerome that 'ignorance of the scriptures is ignorance of Christ.'

> The church has always venerated the divine scriptures as it has venerated the Body of the Lord … It has always regarded and continues to regard the scriptures, taken together with sacred tradition, as the supreme rule of its faith. For, since they are inspired by God and committed to writing once and for all time, they present God's own word in an unalterable form, and they make the voice of the Holy Spirit sound again and again in the words of the prophets and apostles … In the sacred books the Father who is in heaven comes lovingly to meet his children, and talks with them.[8]

The Word of God plays an important role in the lives of associates. At the very core of the contemporary expression of spirituality is the Word of God. It is in contemplating Christ in the gospels that the associates become more conformed to the image of Christ, grow in holiness and understand more profoundly the charism of their particular congregation. Various institutes have their favourite texts on Christian or biblical themes that help to form and express their spirituality. It is by listening to and pondering the word that they will be transformed and renewed. By being in tune with and reflecting the ongoing liturgical cycle, the whole mystery of salvation is unfolded before them in an ongoing way. In the introduction to the *Liturgy of the Hours* (The Divine Office) we are told:

> The reading is not the result of individual choice or devotion but is the planned decision of the church itself, in order that

in the course of the year the Bride of Christ may unfold the mystery of Christ from his incarnation and birth until his ascension and the expectation of blessed hope and of the Lord's return.[9]

All the great classics of spirituality emphasise the bible. It is the prime source of spiritual growth: 'All scripture is inspired by God and can profitably be used for teaching, for refuting error, for guiding people's lives and teaching them to be holy' (2 Tim 3:16).

We cannot, however, expect that the word of God will automatically effect changes in us. We need preparation to receive what the Eastern Churches call 'God's love-letter to his people'. This will involve some basic understanding of what the bible is and how it is written. But it is more important to try to allow the scriptures to become a living word. The actualisation of the word of God in concrete living needs the grace of the Holy Spirit. A prayerful discernment and openness becomes a necessary preparation for reading the word.

Liturgical Prayer

One of the great rediscoveries after Vatican II was the beauty of the *Liturgy of the Hours*. This was, of course, facilitated by a deep revision of the text of the Divine Office and the provision of texts in the vernacular. The *Liturgy of the Hours* is not a prayer book restricted to priests and religious. The Council in its Constitution on Sacred Liturgy, *Sacrosanctum concilium*, described the *Liturgy of the Hours* as the prayer of the whole people of God.

> The Divine Office, in keeping with ancient tradition, is so devised that the whole course of the day and night is consecrated by the praise of God. Therefore, when this wonderful song of praise is correctly celebrated by priests and others deputed for this purpose by the church's ordinance, or by the faithful praying together with the priest, then it is truly the voice of the bride herself addressed to the bridegroom. And what is more, it is the prayer which Christ himself together with his body addresses to the Father.[10]

Pope Paul VI in his Apostolic Constitution, *Laudis canticum*, further developed the ideas of the council.

Now that the prayer of holy church has been reformed and entirely revised in keeping with its very ancient tradition and in light of the needs of our day, it is to be hoped above all that the *Liturgy of the Hours* may penetrate the whole of Christian prayer, giving it life, direction, and expression and effectively nourishing the spiritual life of the people of God ... Christian prayer above all is the prayer of the whole community, which Christ joins to himself. Everyone shares in this prayer, which is proper to the one Body as it offers prayers that give expression to the voice of Christ's beloved Bride, to the hopes and desires the whole Christian people.[11]

These sentiments would become realities only when the office books were translated. Before the council the difficult Latin of the Breviary was a blockage to its being a source for spiritual insight. Its recitation by priests and some religious was a true act of worship, even if at times its recitation may have been painful and unenlightening.

Later in Paul VI's Constitution we have the beautiful statement:

The whole life of the faithful, hour by hour during day and night, is a kind of *leitourgia* or public service, in which the faithful give themselves over to the ministry of love towards God and neighbour, identifying themselves with the action of Christ, who by his life and self-offering sanctified the life of all humanity. The *Liturgy of the Hours* clearly expresses and effectively strengthens this sublime truth, embodied in the Christian life. For this reason the hours are recommended to all Christ's faithful members.[12]

One might add that many lay people appreciate the liturgical hours of Morning and Evening Prayer, even though one hears of priests and religious who think that it is too complex for laity. The book in the hand becomes a reliable friend, ready for daily celebration in the middle of busy lay lives.

Robert Taft in his book *The Liturgy of the Hours in East and West* calls the *Liturgy of the Hours* the church's school of prayer because it is a biblical, objective, traditional prayer. It is mainly the Word of God from both the Old and New Testaments. No other form of prayer is so rooted in the mysteries of salvation history as they unfold day by day in the church's annual cycle.[13] It is a canticle of praise, unceasingly hymned in heaven and brought into this world of ours by our High Priest Jesus Christ and faithfully continued by his church throughout the ages, though in a variety of forms.[14]

Morning and Evening Prayer of the church is a very excellent form of prayer for all God's people, especially for associate members who are zooming in on the tradition of a religious congregation. Morning Prayer is designed and structured to sanctify the beginning of the day. It is a preparation for the day, and as the sun rises so too minds and hearts are lifted up to the resurrection of the Lord. The theme of Morning Prayer is 'light'. Evening Prayer is a prayer of thanksgiving, our evening sacrifice in union with Christ's death on the cross, a prayer for the light of Christ, and a prayer of praise to the Holy Trinity.[15] It is said to-wards the end of the day, as the light fades and evening is upon us. It is a way of giving thanks for the day that is over and for work well done.

In the psalms we use the very word of God to praise God. We allow the Spirit to form his prayer in our heart (see Rom 8:26-27). The psalms are in a perfect sense 'the prayer of Christ'. They contain not only the ancient promises which Christ himself came to fulfill, but they show forth everywhere the glory of Jesus, his supreme and eternal power as king and priest. With Christ those praying the psalms are drawn into and join in

> that hymn which is sung throughout all ages in the realms above. He joins the entire community of humankind to him-self, associating it with himself in singing his divine song of praise.[16]

Morning and Evening prayer, the 'two hinges of the *Liturgy of the Hours*' join the associates to heaven and anticipate the day in which all creation will be healed. The daily hours are a major discovery for associates and a key enrichment in their lives.

Devotion to Mary
Devotion to Mary will play a key part in the spirituality of assoc-iates, especially where the congregation has developed a Marian devotion. The associate members will be called to radiate in their everyday life the *fiat*, the 'yes' of Mary.

The Second Vatican Council, after much debate, placed the document on Mary within the context of the Constitution on the Church, *Lumen gentium,* showing clearly the role Mary is to have within the church. Chapter eight of *Lumen gentium* opens with a reminder that the reason why Christians ought to reverence the memory of Mary is that it is through her the Son of God came into our history.

When the fullness of time had come, God sent his Son, born of a woman, born under the law, in order to redeem those who were under the law, so that we might receive adoption as children. (Gal 4:4)

Her assent to the incarnation was required and having said 'yes' she devoted herself totally, as handmaid of the Lord, to the person and work of her Son. She did not have a passive role but she 'freely co-operated in the work of human salvation through faith and obedience.'[17] With the Annunciation Mary began a pilgrimage of faith that would bring her to the foot of the cross.[18] Mary freely accepted God's invitation to be the mother of Jesus. She had to have the faith and the courage to be open to the favour that God was bestowing on her. It is as a woman of faith that Mary is blessed.

Blessed is she who believed that the promise made her by the Lord would be fulfilled. (Lk 1: 45)

Mary's journey of faith did not become easier with the birth of Jesus. At each stage she knew the darkness of faith. After the visit of the angel she did not seem to have received any further messengers but had to go on the little light she had received. What must have been her thoughts when she presented Jesus in the temple and there heard the words of Anna and Simeon, when she lost Jesus for three days and found him teaching in the temple? We do not know her feelings throughout his public ministry. We can only guess at her distress in the utter darkness of his death on the cross when we find her there still believing, still saying 'yes' in faith that 'nothing is impossible to God' (Lk 1:37). Truly a model for all associates.

In the church today we can find some problems about Mary. Vatican II warned about excess in devotion. Some people find devotion to Mary difficult. They can be turned off by extremes in the past, by poor presentation of Marian spirituality. We find also concerns in contemporary feminist writings. Others may have a somewhat extravagant attachment to some forms of Marian piety or apparitions. Vatican II shows us the two roles that will keep our devotion sound: 'she occupied a place in the church which is the highest after Christ and closest to us'.[19] The authentic tradition of religious congregations will be a sure guide for Marian devotion. From their religious family, associates will learn how to avoid the two extremes deplored by Vatican II, excess or neglect of the Virgin.[20]

Devotion to the Saints
Devotion to the saints is an important aspect of the Christian life. 'Being more closely united to Christ, those who dwell in heaven consolidate the holiness of the whole church, add to the nobility of the worship that the church offers to God here on earth, and in many ways help in a greater building up of the church' (see 1 Cor 12:12-27).[21] Once received into their heavenly home and being present to the Lord (see 2 Cor 5:8), through him and with him and in him they do not cease to intercede with the Father for us. Many associate groups will have a particular affinity with one saint, either as patron or as founder of the congregation.

The saints are models for Christian living. Indeed great theologians like Hans Urs von Balthasar and Karl Rahner see them as 'creators of new styles of Christianity' or as living commentators on the gospel.[22]

Shared Prayer
Shared prayer with other associates and the religious members of the congregation can be of key importance to associates and to their life and development as associate members. When associates and religious come together to pray, share and reflect on the word of God in *lectio divina* (sacred reading), or some similar method, new richness and insights are gained. Pope John Paul, in his encyclical for the third millennium, spoke highly of *lectio divina* as a method of prayer and recommended it to all God's people. He said that it 'has the potential to enrich not only individuals but the church as a whole.'[23]

There are many advantages in the various forms of shared

prayer. We hear how others pray. We can learn from their prayer and be inspired by it. We also share our own personal relationship with God and support one another in life through prayer.

Private Prayer
Private and personal prayer is of key importance in the life and growth of associate members. It is in setting aside time to be alone with the Lord, to reflect on the attitudes of Jesus in the gospels and on his radical call to repent and believe the good news, that associates will grow in the likeness of Christ and the beatitudes. *The Catechism of the Catholic Church* quotes St Teresa of Avila when it speaks of reflective prayer: 'a close sharing between friends; it means taking time frequently to be alone with him who we know loves us'.[24] Their lives will be transformed and they become more and more conformed to the 'mind of Christ' (Phil 2:2).

Finding or making time for some daily personal prayer can be extremely difficult in our contemporary world. The living wisdom of religious congregations shows that a serious commitment to personal prayer is important and essential for growth in holiness. Religious life also teaches us that excessive time in prayer is not healthy and cannot be sustained. On the other hand, genuine commitment on a regular or even daily basis should be undertaken for a period of time that is realistic. We can all share our struggles, our own habits or opportunities for setting aside time for God. Religious and associates can learn from one another in addressing this challenge of finding time for prayer in a busy and overactive world.

COMMUNITY/FAMILY SPIRIT/ TOGETHERNESS/KOINONIA/MUINTEARAS

In an earlier chapter we have already noted the rich word *koinonia*. It is a vital part of associate membership. Associates are challenged and called to contribute and nurture a sense and experience of community.

The need for Christian Community
In a world often characterised by loneliness and isolation,

associate members are called to be interdependent, caring for one another and drawing on the gifts of one another. In short they are called to a life of communion, *koinonia*, or what is communicated by the Irish word *muintearas* (communityness). If associates are to be people who radiate God's love, compassion and mercy and bring the good news to those they meet, they need to experience and receive love, compassion and mercy as well as sharing these with others.

They receive a heritage or charism. But they will need the help not only of religious, but also of other laity on the same spiritual journey. Associate membership gives them a unique and blessed opportunity to create community, one based on well tested models going back perhaps for centuries.

Community, sign of the loving presence of God
Associates are encouraged and supported by each other and are a sign to all of the loving presence of God, 'a sign and instrument of the communion of God'.[25] As associate members they choose to proclaim the kingdom here on earth, to share their gifts and talents and to support each other in love. The purpose of all community and communion is mission. Associates experience a sense of 'togetherness'. They are part of a larger family, where they can feel accepted and where they can share their hopes and fears. A sense of being valued as associate members gives them a new dignity and feeling of self worth so that they have more confidence in themselves.

Community, a place to share faith
For some people to be associate members of a religious congregation may be the major Christian contact in their lives. At the associate gatherings, with individual associates or with members of the congregation, they can share their faith journeys in confidence and trust. Through associate membership there is always someone there for them in times of need. There is someone to listen, to support them through their difficulties and rejoice with them in their good times. In the day-in-day-out struggle of living Christian values in a world whose values can be far from Christian, associate membership is a tremendous support and reassurance that only in God and in the things of God is there

peace and love. Often associates have been given confidence, courage and strength to hang in there when the going gets tough because of the example or encouragement of a member of the congregation or an associate. Associate membership provides a unique and especially graced opportunity for them to grow in love of God and others. As they meet with the members of the congregation and other associates, who are like minded and who share their enthusiasm for gospel values, they can experience the warmth of friendship, compassion and understanding so as to be drawn to reflect these values in their own lives.

Community, a place to go from to spread the good news
It is by being strengthened in community that the associates can go out and proclaim the good news of Jesus. At the very beginning of his earthly ministry, Jesus gathered a group of disciples around him. They supported each other by praying, sharing, eating, working together. They went to quiet places where they could be alone together, drawing strength from each other. So too as the associates meet together to pray, share and support each other, they are given courage to go out to proclaim the kingdom, to spread the good news in their homes and places of work.

Mission / Ministry / Social Concern

There is always a danger of even the best things being used selfishly. Spirituality is no exception. The spiritual traditions and the lives of the saints show that holiness can not be a comfy relationship between me and God. It is not a selfish quest, but has to be open to others. A most important element of associate membership is mission or ministry. Vatican II and the subsequent documents of Paul VI and John Paul II firmly established the missionary nature of the lives of all the People of God. Throughout the documents of Vatican II the term 'ministry' and 'minister' are used for the clergy and the mission of the laity is usually described as the 'apostolate'. These two words 'mission' and 'ministry' are often confused. There is a tendency to interchange them in everyday use. Therefore it is important to take a general look at their meaning.

Mission

Mission is a word that has been used in a variety of ways. Its Latin root implies someone who is sent out with a message to another. Through baptism and confirmation Christians are missioned, sent by Christ into the world to proclaim the good news of salvation in continuity with his own mission. Any theology of the laity, as of the ordained priesthood or of religious life, has to begin from the basic idea of a mission flowing from baptism and confirmation. How members of these three different states within the church live, and what they do, is determined by the specific way in which they share the mission of the church.

Vatican II firmly established the missionary nature of the lives of all the People of God in baptism. We have already noted the statement of *Lumen gentium* 31:

> All the Faithful, that is, who by baptism are incorporated into Christ are constituted the people of God, who have been made sharers in their own way in the priestly, prophetic and kingly office of Christ and play their part in carrying out the mission of the whole Christian people in the church and in the world.[26]

Later in the same document we find:

> The apostolate of the laity is a sharing in the church's saving mission. Through baptism and confirmation all are appointed to this apostolate by the Lord himself ... The laity, however are given this special vocation: to make the church present and fruitful in those places and circumstances where it is only through them that it can become the salt of the earth. Thus all lay people, through the gifts which they have received, are at once the witnesses and the living instruments of the mission of the church itself 'according to the measure of Christ's gift'. (Eph 4:7)[27]

The Decree on the apostolate of the laity also sees the apostolate of the laity as a sharing in the mission of the church. Lay people in carrying out this mission will exercise their apostolate both in the church and in the world.[28] All are called to mission through baptism and confirmation. The call to individual holiness is inseparably linked to mission. Growth in holiness brings with it the desire to bear a living witness to the good news of salvation.

Thus holiness and mission go hand in hand:

> All who have been baptised have put on the person of Christ and form one person in him. (Gal 3:27-28) … You are a chosen race, a royal priesthood, a holy nation, a people set apart to sing the praises of God (1 Pet 2:9-10).

Ministry

We now come to ministry (from *minus*, meaning less or lesser). The minister is the one who renders service or aid, a servant. Ministry is something that marks one out as a servant of the person or people to whom one is sent.

Vatican II went some way in developing the notion of 'ministry' which up to then was almost exclusively confined to the activity of the hierarchy. The 1983 Code of Canon Law used the word 'apostolate', where Vatican II often used the word 'ministry' to cover all aspects of the church's mission. In it lay ministries are divided into two types of functions: (1) liturgical or pastoral, which are a participation of the laity in the ordained ministry and (2) those which do not originate from the ordained ministry and require a special mission from the hierarchy in order to be exercised in favour of the Christian community.

The post-synodal apostolic exhortation, *Christifideles laici*, gave a further clarity to the notion of ministry, stating that some ministries come from the sacrament of orders, while others come from baptism and confirmation and belong to all the faithful. An issue in recent years has been some confusion between ministries which are proper to ordained ministers only, and those that can be undertaken by lay ministers.[29]

T. O'Meara, in his book *Theology of Ministry*, defines Christian ministry as:

> the public activity of a baptised follower of Jesus Christ flowing from the Spirit's charism and an individual personality on behalf of a Christian community witness to serve and realise the kingdom of God.[30]

O'Meara earlier clarifies this definition by stating that ministry has six characteristics: '1) doing something, 2) for the coming of the Kingdom, 3) in public, 4) on behalf of a Christian community, 5) which is a gift received in faith, baptism and ordination and which is 6) an activity with its own limits and identity within a diversity of ministerial actions.'[31]

However, Christopher O'Donnell argues that what specifies ministry in the church is the giving of a charism by the Spirit to a person and its regular use by that person in service. He claims that ministry is involved, when for example, somebody with a charism for visiting elderly people in their homes, quietly uses this gift with few being aware of it.

While O'Meara's definition of ministry and its six character-istics can be applied to the ministry of associates, it is also clear that in many instances associates are quietly acting as Christ's hands or feet, ministering in his name without anyone being aware other than the person to whom they are ministering to. Therefore O' Donnell's definition is perhaps more helpful in de-scribing the ministries of associates. It has, however, a weakness in perhaps diluting excessively the notion of ministry so that any activity might be called ministry.

Lay associate membership of a religious congregation can be a powerful stimulus in helping lay people to come to an under-standing that through their baptismal consecration they share in the life and love of the Trinity and are called to live in holiness, by living the Christian vocation to the full. Associate members are called to proclaim the kingdom of God on earth, to share their gifts and talents and to support each other in a loving way. They are also missioned to live their Christian commitment in a simple lifestyle, inspired by the beatitudes. They should have a basic attitude of openness to, and reconciliation with others, aware that differences of culture and background, far from di-viding them, are a revelation of the infinite diversity of God's creative love. Their fidelity to gospel values makes them a sign of hope, enabling them to witness to the presence of Christ in the world. Following Christ's example they seek to live in sensitivity to the cry of the poor, listening and responding to the word of God and the needs of the world. In a world marked by poverty, hunger and destitution, associates are called to witness to God's loving kindness as revealed in Christ. They assume a prophetic role in fostering social justice. In all of this they draw on the in-sights into mission and ministry of their religious families. These general exhortations and values will be found incarnated in religious institutes. Each religious institute has had its own specific ministries. Some of these arose from the needs of society.

In time these ministries were taken over by other groups in society or other bodies took over the provision for needs in the areas of health, education and social deprivation. This has posed a problem for religious who may now see little room for their historic ministry. This change can lead to a loss of identity, to a decline in vocations, to a lowering of morale. Lay associates, like the contemporary religious, have to discern what the essence of a particular charism or ministry is. This core gift will in many cases have to be given new expressions in the religious institutes and be appropriated by the associate members in their secular environment.

COMMITMENT / RESPONSE

In a society where stability is lessening, where many aspects of society may be dysfunctional, and people shy away from any form of commitment, the witness of associate members publicly making a response (commitment) is a striking counter witness. In a world where God is often forgotten, where people can be ignored or trampled on, associates dedicate themselves to living a life of love and service in their homes, places of work, in parish activities, in furthering the kingdom of God in the world. Above all, associate membership is a commitment to live out our baptismal consecration; it is a call to holiness in prayer and service in the varied circumstances of our lives.

The commitment or response is always in an attitude of openness and humility. It involves a deep realisation of the dignity of all people. Associates learn that they can receive insight, inspiration and help from each other. It is in the realisation of their own weakness and need of the love and mercy of God that they can make a commitment/response.

In a diverse world associates recognise that all things are God's creation. They see how greed and exploitation may damage the environment. As associates they commit themselves to care for the earth and its resources and to share with others what they have received as gift. What the world needs today are people who offer an alternative witness – a witness of hope, love and compassion; people who will show another way, another route which will bring peace and healing. Above all people need meaning for their lives and some answers, even if inadequate ones, to the problems of suffering and death.

We have already seen that in third orders there were vows or latterly promises. Each association will have its own form of commitment which will reflect something of the spirituality and traditions of the religious congregation. There can be different lengths of commitment. Associates usually make some initial commitment for one or three years. They then make a more formal commitment for life (or until revoked).

Some features of associate commitments are generally common. They enshrine a promise to God to live a more dedicated life according to the spiritual traditions of a religious family. The legislation or way of life proposed to associates may be more or less demanding. Ideally the commitment is not seen as a burden but as a way of life which gives inner peace and true freedom. It is a guide for living and supports the number of fresh decisions that have to be made in the spiritual life. It is, especially, a reminder of what is important in the Christian response to work, mission and service. Some people, especially the young, have problems with long-term commitment. A throw-away society sees value only in what is useful. A commitment to institutes and values to be lived in an unknown future is daunting for many people.

FORMATION

One of the very important aspects of associate membership is the formation of members. It is of vital importance that associates are formed to take their rightful place in the church, that they understand their role and mission in the church. Vatican II documents, many post-conciliar documents and *The Catechism of the Catholic Church* (1994)[32] speak of the role of the laity in the church and the world.

As associates members of a religious congregation people have opportunity to study these documents. We have seen that the document on consecrated life (*Vita consecrata*) makes special mention of associate membership. Pope John Paul II wrote that when laity have opportunities to participate in associate programmes:

they often bring unexpected and rich insights into certain aspects of the charism leading to a more spiritual interpretation of it, and helping to draw from it directions for new activities in the apostolate.

In the whole process of associates and religious meeting together to pray, to share, to have ongoing input on topics relevant to their lives as associates, the associates are formed in attitudes of the church and Christian living. They have opportunity to become aware of the importance of the secular nature of their vocation.

It is essential that each associate group draws up its own associate formation programme.

There are several dimensions to a good formation programme. Firstly, people can learn the acquired wisdom of a religious family. This can guide people about prayer or appropriate penance. Secondly, there is the question of the nature and intensity of the formation that may be needed. This will depend on the culture of the people, their education, their spiritual gifts etc. Formation programmes need to be flexible. Thirdly, we can distinguish two areas of intellectual formation. People need to know the four main contents of *The Catechism of the Catholic Church*. The whole book itself may not initially be found helpful, but committed Catholics should know about the four main sections of the catechism: 1) Profession of faith; 2) The celebration of the Christian Mystery; 3) Life in Christ; 4) Christian prayer. Some people coming to associate meetings will need more or less help with this material.

Another element of intellectual formation will include the history and writings of the religious institute. The insights of founders, and of significant persons in the congregation will help in the formation of the candidates in the spirit of associate membership.

Fourthly, there are non-intellectual areas of formation. Here the old adage may be adopted: the charism or spirit will be caught rather than taught. It is through experience, through living contact with other associates and religious, that gradually the vision of associate membership is communicated in life rather than merely set down in documents, no matter how worthy.

It is the experience of many lay associations that getting a formation programme right is essential for fruitful growth. The influence of a parent congregation is vital. The religious are, after all, bearers of the charism. But the charism is not static. It is developing anew in lay spirituality. This is an area in which the religious will not have the last or even the most important word. There is need for dialogue between religious and laity that is on both sides open, respectful and humble.

LEGISLATION / ESSENTIAL STRUCTURES

We might ask, why law? Laws lay down do's and don'ts. Very often they come about through difficulties. We find a problem that gives rise to a law, which in turn can lead to peace and order. St Paul was a teacher and guide at Corinth. The church there was very charismatic but its assemblies were very disordered; a large problem was prophecy. Paul sorted it out: he said that two or three prophets could speak (see 1 Cor 14:26-33). There is no absolute reason for two or three prophets as against one or two, or even three or four. It was a practical judgement that allowed the church to meet and worship in an orderly way.

Usually when groups get bigger we feel a need for order. A meeting of more than six will generally function better with a guide, chairperson or facilitator. The whole point of law is order; law enables reasonable people to co-operate. In some countries people drive on the left side of the road, in others on the right. It does not matter which, provided that people agree and obey the law.

Another point of law is to protect values. The Eucharistic fast is meant to inculcate respect for the Body of the Lord; the Sunday Mass obligation is imposed to protect and show how in practice the third commandment on the Sabbath is to be observed; the demand for the minimum age for marriage or priesthood is to ensure some requisite maturity.

Over the years religious life developed rules. At first there were hermits living apart in the desert; later there were some loose bonds with a spiritual leader. But unless there are rules people cannot know how much is expected. Hence the great Rules (Augustine, Benedict, Basil, Albert) laid down spiritual principles as well as norms for the conduct of life. In addition to such Rules, customs develop. People try something out. If it serves the group then it can become a custom and later even a law.

The Twentieth Century

We have seen in previous chapters that in 1917 a code or a comprehensive unified body of law was given to the church for the first time. Before that time legislation was scattered in a huge number of places and sources. The 1917 Code was to serve the church well for half a century. It tended to be quite detailed about religious congregations, with many do's and don'ts. It was a collection of practical norms, with little inspirational material. When it was produced there was little theology, much less spirituality, of the laity. The vision of the 1917 Code was both clerical and legalistic.

Again, as we indicated previously, in the 1920s the church began to experience vibrant lay movements like the St Vincent de Paul which did not fit into the existing static categories of clerics, religious and laity. As we saw, the notion of association developed more widely in the church.

With Vatican II the church welcomed a new rich theology of both religious life and laity. All religious bodies had to write constitutions, that is legislation for themselves. The difference compared with 1917 was that constitutions not only had to state what was to be done but also why. Constitutions were to be spiritual and inspirational as well as setting legal norms.

The new 1983 Code of Canon Law demanded revision of constitutions or legislation at every level. When it comes to the writing of constitutions there can be a variety of approaches to law and legislation. Some people are almost allergic to law and regulations; they feel that law ties down spontaneity and they prefer freedom; some want legislation to be short and clear; some want everything spelled out; some are impatient with spirituality and inspirational material in legal texts; most insist on law being practical; some have a horror of repetition; some do not like symbolic language, others are averse to theoretical expressions.

In the case of religious institutes which are international there should be an acquired wisdom which allows a different expression according to country and cultures. These institutes may have constitutions for whole congregations and subsidiary norms often called statutes for different countries, provinces and regions. Legislation for associates will also need to be sensitive to different regions.

Normally the constitutions are in two parts. The first part is spiritual, reflecting the charism, spirituality and mission of congregations which can be endlessly reflected upon in prayer. The second part is practical and legislative; it can be regarded as informative, explaining what the congregation needs to know about itself and the way it operates. Constitutions or legislations are not written in granite for ever. They can be modified and renewed at a General Assembly or Chapter of the congregation.

It is of vital importance that associates of a religious congregation have some form of legislation that reflects the charism, spirituality, mission of the parent congregation. They also need to have some form of guidelines that inform and direct the autonomy of the group and the link between the congregation and associates.

Problems can arise when there is no such legislation. People need to know how one becomes an associate, what are the rights and obligations, how one ceases to be an associate. Where there is inadequate legislation, problems may emerge which can be divisive.

Legislation must also indicate the right relationships between associates and the parent institute. The associate members may have too much independence from the religious. This can lead to a watering down of the charism etc. Others can be too dependent on the congregation. The religious may not trust the associate members enough. There is need for prayerful reflection and ongoing dialogue between the religious and associates so that it is truly a lay associate group of a religious congregation. The balance between associates and religious must always be held in tension. Associate membership is a partnership between associates and religious.

Conclusion
This chapter has looked at some key elements that one would expect in a developed lay associate membership of a religious

congregation. There will be other elements or aspects arising from the specific charism of the institute. However, not all institutes at the present time have reached this level of development. Many are at initial stages of gathering people for prayer and discussion. They may not know the outcome of these first steps but it would seem very important even at the beginning to have genuine dialogue which reflects the actual nature of both religious and lay life.

FURTHER READING

Church Documents

The Catechism of the Catholic Church, 'The Communion of the Church of Heaven and Earth,'(Dublin: Veritas Publications, 1994) nn 954-959

Pope Paul VI, Apostolic Exhortation, Evangelisation in the Modern World, *Evangelii nuntiandi*, (London, Catholic Truth Society, 1975).

Books and Articles

V. Cosstick, 'Formation and the Koinonia Church,' *The Way* 33 (1990) 188-198.

B. Grogan, 'Lay Community and Church Survival,' *Religious Life Review* 31(1992) 179-183.

E. Malasesta, 'Charism', *The New Dictionary of Catholic Spirituality*, ed M. Downey (Collegeville: The Liturgical Press, 1993) 140-143

P. Mullins, 'The Theology of Charisms: Vatican II and the New Catechism,' *Milltown Studies* 33 (1994) 123-162.

W. J. Rademacher, *Lay Ministry, A Theological, Spiritual & Pastoral Handbook* (Slough, St Paul Publications, 1991)

A. A. Hagstrom, *The Concepts of the Vocation and the Mission of the Laity* (San Francisco-London, 1994)

NOTES

1. See Vatican II, Church, *LG* 6, 4 and 12
2. *LG* 12
3. *PO* 9
4. *AA* 3

5. *PO* 2

6. See 'Apostolic Exhortation on the Renewal of Religious Life', *Evangelica testificatio* (1971)

7. The Constitution on the Liturgy (*Sacrosanctum concilium*) 48

8. *DV* 21

9. General Instruction on the Liturgy of the Hours 140

10. *SC* 84

11. *Laudis canticum* (1971) 8

12. Ibid

13. Robert Taft, *The Liturgy of the Hours in East and West*, (Collegeville: Liturgical Press, 1986) 368.

14. Introduction to *Laudis Canticum*

15. See General Instructions of the Liturgy of the Hours 37, 39-54

16. *SC* 83

17. *LG* 56

18. See *LG* 58

19. *LG* 54

20. *LG* 67

21. *LG* 49

22. C. O'Donnell, articles, 'Saints' and 'Theological Sources' in *Ecclesia : A Theological Encyclopedia of the Church*, (Collegeville: The Liturgical Press, 1996) 416-417; 443-444.

23. Pope John Paul II, Apostolic Letter, *Novo millennio ineunte*, (letter at the close of the Great Jubilee, the year, 2000) n 39

24. *The Catechism of the Catholic Church* n.27

25. Code of Canon Law (1983) n 780

26. *LG* 31

27. *LG* 33

28. *AA* 5

29. *CL* 32

30. *LG* 33

31. *CL* 32

32. 136

33. *Vita consecrata* 55

CHAPTER SIX

Associate Membership: A Contribution to Lay Spirituality and the Church

We began this book by considering the notion of spirituality and lay spirituality in particular. We considered how in the past the church has worked from a position of control and dominance which led to the laity being often treated as second-class members of the church. We saw how towards the end of the reign of Pope Pius XII there was the beginning of an air of expectancy among some laity in the church and key theologians of the period such as Yves Congar and Karl Rahner.

The Signs of the Times
In 1957, Pius XII spoke of a new springtime in the church. In 1958 he was succeeded by Pope John XXIII who a year later announced Vatican II, praying for 'a new Pentecost' in the church. He spoke of the importance of the church being attentive to the 'signs of the times' and finding an adequate expression for its message so that it will be understood by the people of the time. Foremost in the mind of John XXIII was to make the church relevant to the people of the modern world and to open its doors to renewal, to *aggiornamento*.

At the beginning of the new millennium and at the end of the Great Jubilee year, Pope John Paul in his apostolic letter, 'At the Start of the New Millennium', (*Novo millennio ineunte*) spoke of the encouragement and hope that comes from being led by the risen Lord and the inexhaustible power of the Spirit always bringing about new surprises and gifts for the church

Church Guidance
We have seen that the Vatican II documents, the Dogmatic Constitution on the Church, *Lumen gentium*, the Decree on the Apostolate of the Laity, *Apostolicam actuositatem*, as well as the subsequent 1983 Code of Canon Law and the Apostolic

Exhortation on the Vocation and Mission of the Laity in the Church and in the World, *Christifideles laici*, made significant contributions on the subject of the laity, on who they are and on their role and place in the church. Many fruits and blessings for the laity and for the church have come about through the ecclesiological insights of these documents:

- a deeper understanding and appreciation of the equality and dignity of the laity as belonging to the People of God through baptism.
- the universal call to holiness.
- a fundamental right of all to share and play their part in the mission of the church as sharers in the priestly, prophetic and kingly office of Christ.
- their unique role in the mission of the church because of their secular character.
- The sacraments of baptism and confirmation, and charisms equipping all and empowering them for mission

We have then documents which gave great encouragement to the development and spirituality of laity. We have seen the achievements and limitations of documents of Vatican II and afterwards.

SOME KEY PROBLEMS IN THE DEVELOPMENT OF A MATURE LAITY

We turn then to the key elements of lay associate membership of a religious congregation that we examined in the previous chapter and look at areas requiring study or reflection.

Development of a spirituality

The recent exhortation of John Paul II on the Church in Europe gave a sober analysis of the problems of our time.[1] He sought, however, to look beyond them in Christian hope. We can identify needs of the laity and can indicate that associate membership of a religious congregation can show up other needs.

One of the 'signs of the times' in today's world among people is a search, a hunger for God, for a spirituality that has meaning and relevance for their lives. This can be seen in the growth of New Age and occult practices, where people are looking for someone or something to fill the void in their lives. Many people are interested in spirituality, but have difficulty in understanding such matters as God, Christ, church, or morality. Such spirituality can be a self-seeking, endless search with new forms constantly sought, tried and dropped. Others are highly qualified in their professions but still have a childish, immature understanding of faith and have had no real training in developing an adult spirituality or relationship with God. Yet others, who are fully committed to their parish and who have recognised the call of all Christians to holiness, and have developed their faith and prayer life alongside their professional life are, however, often dissatisfied with the support structures available to them. They live in a harsh secular environment; their friends and colleagues do not share their religious or even human values. The church often does not seem to offer what they need; indeed people may be unable to articulate their deepest desires or needs. They do not find adequate opportunities for spiritual growth in liturgies, homilies or in parish groups; these do not seem relevant to their life in the world. What is offered at parish level is generally aimed at the 'average' person, with little being available for those who want a deeper experience of church. This can lead to discouragement and frustration. This may be the result of lack of leadership on the part of the clergy, but equally it may be due to a reluctance of the laity to take seriously their role in the mission of the church and to provide faith support groups for each other. It is of utmost importance that the prayer life of the laity is developed. Pope John Paul II in his millennium letter *Novo millennio ineunte* speaks of the need to train people in the art of prayer. Prayer cannot be taken for granted. People need to be taught to celebrate and speak to God, to learn how to listen to him and develop a personal relationship with him.[2] Prayer is gift of the Spirit but it also needs to be learned. Spirituality is needed to harmonise prayer and to give meaning to the concrete reality of life in the world lived by mature Christians.

We turn then to the key elements of lay associate membership of a religious congregation that we examined in the previous chapter, and look to possible or necessary further study or reflection.

The development of a community
A major problem in the church today is a weakness of community. The church has in some respects over-sacramentalised people at the expense of evangelising them and creating fellowship or community. It has in many ways failed to build community. Many people today are looking for a much deeper type of belonging to the church and a deeper sense of community. Indeed one of the scandals of the church today is its failure to provide a church community that is truly inclusive. One of the greatest challenges facing the church is to go beyond individualism and to promote a spirituality of communion. As Pope John Paul II states in *Novo millennio ineunte*:

> A spirituality of communion indicates above all the heart's contemplation of the mystery of the Trinity dwelling in us, and whose light we must also be able to see shining on the face of the brothers and sisters around us.[3]

This leads to the question of how community is to come about and this in turn brings up the issue of charism because, as we have seen, renewal is primarily a work of the Spirit.

Mission/Ministry/Social Concern
There is the question of mission on which there has been much insistence at Vatican II, in *Evangelii nuntiandi* (1975) as well as in the later *Christifideles laici* (1988). Since the Second Vatican Council opened the way to greater participation of all God's people in the life and mission of the church, the laity have been involved in a variety of ministries and participation in the liturgy which in the past seemed the sole preserve of the clergy. However, the position of the vast majority of the laity remains unchanged, the new involvement offered by Vatican Two being for the most part restricted to a committed minority operating within the church structures, most of which still remain clerical. Today we have Eucharistic Ministers, readers, spiritual directors, pastoral teams, theologians etc. Yet it seems that the vast majority of the laity have little sense of their identity as church. They have not participated to any great extent in the priestly, prophetic and royal offices of Christ. They have failed to understand their baptismal call to participate in the church's mission

and the secular nature of that vocation. The notion that the church through the laity has a secular dimension, has been little discussed in the years since the council, thus depriving the church of an important element of its inner life and its relationship with the world. A consequence has been a decrease in the effectiveness of the laity in the mission of the church. Whilst it is clear that the laity have to be involved in the mission of the church, it is not nearly so clear how.

There is a further point that runs right through the church, namely marginalisation. This is of two kinds. There are some who indeed feel isolated and marginalised from the church for reasons such as moral precepts like contraception, Vatican pronouncements about the role of women, irregular extra-marital relationships, unfortunate experiences of the institutional church. But there are also people who are more profoundly isolated and marginalised and do not even know it: they do not see the relevance of the church for the important issues of their lives. There is then an urgent need within the church today to form lay people in a theology appropriate to their situation, to explain church teaching and encourage them to participate actively in spirituality, community experiences and ministry.

Beneath each of the above needs, problems or difficulties there are important challenges and opportunities. While there are indeed many among both pastors and laity who have shown themselves to be aware of these problems, one cannot feel overly impressed with the solutions to date. There will of course be many possibilities, each with its own emphasis, focus, strengths and weaknesses. But the concern of this book is to look at one type of solution which provides some structures and makes a significant contribution to the church and lay spirituality, namely lay associate membership of religious congregations. As previously stated, associate membership is also a response of religious congregations to the 'signs of the times', a new openness to the laity and a willingness of religious to share their charisms, spirituality and mission with the laity. In a certain sense, religious congregations are taking seriously the mandate of *Perfectae caritatis* for religious to return again to their founding charism. We will now turn to associate membership of a religious congregation to discover how in its key elements of charism, spirituality, community, mission and commitment there is a response to this challenge and a contribution to the church and to a lay spirituality.

Charism

Charisms are gifts of the Spirit to the church and belong primarily to the people of God as a whole and therefore cannot be claimed by anyone or any group in the church as exclusively belonging to them. Charisms are found throughout the church but we need to be aware of different kinds of charism and different ways in which the Spirit continually sanctifies the church (see *LG* 4). Thus we have clusters of charisms that are characteristic of religious groups. Then we can have further charisms bestowed on the religious community, such as a commitment to oversee evangelisation, justice and peace, or a new outreach to the laity.

In this book we see associate membership as charismatic, drawing laity to the heritage of a particular congregation, itself charismatic. We are talking therefore of the charism of a religious congregation being shared by laity who have their own charisms. This sharing of charisms leads to an enrichment of the charisms rather than a weakening. When the charisms of religious and of lay people are put to together, the Christian witness becomes more consistent and ministry more effective. Through their charisms, members of religious congregations witness to a particular aspect of the gospel message.

One cannot predict or circumscribe charism. Contemporary experience of lay associate members points to an enrichment of religious charism through the insights of the laity, a growth of maturity in laity through encounter with a religious charism and finally a deepened understanding of the charism from those religious who seek to present it to lay people. In a recent book on priestly spirituality D. J. O' Leary notes:

> Compassion moves outwards. It will not be trapped into individual soul saving. It grows only when given away and it can only happen in community. It is a reaching out kind of virtue that is forever purified in the sharing. And it enriches the giver, because there is a sense in which our redeeming compassion is directed towards ourselves ... To be compassionate is to have a heart that suffers from the misfortune of others because we think it is our own.[4]

Associate members are prompted through associate membership and formation to reach out in love and compassion to the church and the world. Thus the church has been blessed as the associate members bring mercy and compassion, healing and enlightenment, caring and encouragement. The associates are a presence, a witness to those around, a sign of what the church must be, if it is to have relevance for people's lives. As mentioned already, people have been alienated from the church, from sharing Eucharist, through some church teachings. Often before people are ready for sacraments, it is a compassionate face of the church that they need. Religious congregations, in sharing their charism with associate members, who in turn are sharing it in their families, workplaces, society, with the broken, alienated and marginalised of society, are making an enormous contribution to and collaboration in the mission of the church.

Spirituality
We have already examined in some detail spirituality in general and the notion of a lay spirituality. What concerns us in this section is the contribution that associate membership of a religious congregation is making to lay spirituality and the church. A main criterion in looking at the contribution of associate membership to a lay spirituality is how far it fosters spiritual maturity, encourages growth in holiness, and supports leadership in families, work place, society and the church. Associate membership has a positive role in fostering a mature and balanced spirituality. It gives associate members an opportunity to rediscover the significance of chapter five of the Constitution on the Church, dedicated to 'The Universal Call to Holiness'. Associate membership provides a rich means of helping lay people to mature and grow in their prayer life and faith. It provides a 'genuine training in holiness, adapted to people's needs'.[5]

This training must integrate the resources offered to everyone with both the traditional forms of individual and group assistance, as well as the more recent forms of support offered in associations.[6]

Above all, it gives to associate members a vision centred on Jesus Christ as Universal King, High Priest of the New and Eternal

Covenant. They are united in joining in the unending hymn of praise to God the Father that goes on day and night in heaven and on earth.

Associate members are given help, encouragement, direction and the inspiration of both religious and associates to develop a spirituality which has meaning for their lives. Associate membership can provide opportunities for people to meet their spiritual needs. The spiritual and formation programme of associates allows these needs to be met and challenges people where they are at. There is a real opportunity to educate associate members in prayer. They have opportunities to be educated in liturgical prayer and to consecrate and direct their day with the recitation of the Prayer of the Church, especially Lauds and Vespers.[7]

We repeat that lay people can find in a religious heritage a spirituality that is balanced and has stood the test of time. Among religious and associates there are many people trained and competent in giving spiritual direction, orientation and input. Such guidance is not usually available at parish level. Obviously this is not to lay blame on busy parishes where there are pressing needs of many kinds; it is rather to see associate membership of a religious community as a contribution to the church and to the development of a lay spirituality. Religious in partnership with the laity can 'point the way towards the future face of the church'.[8] Religious have a long tradition of working with lay people and have developed rich insights which can foster a lay spirituality. A greater sense of trust can be built up and, through growing together with religious, associate members are encouraged and challenged to travel further in their journey of faith than they might without the support system. They have opportunity to share more openly their relationship with God without fear of embarrassment. Often when associates experience praying with scripture through *lectio divina* or other scriptural prayer, their lives are transformed. A life centred on Christ involves constantly reflecting on scripture, fulfilling the exhortation of Vatican II to know the 'surpassing knowledge of Jesus Christ' (Philippians 3:8). The associates have opportunity for theological and biblical studies. They can come into a new understanding of the Eucharist and what it means to be a member of the church. Thus the life of the church is renewed, invigorated and strengthened by their Christian witness. Associate spirituality must meet people where they are, in the ordinary circumstances of their lives, married, single, widowed, separated. It is in family life, at work in the office, school, factory, unemployed, retired, sick that they must have a living spirituality. Spirituality is ultimately communitarian, stressing that all things belong to God and that associates individually and as a body are accountable for the use of the earth's resources. Associate membership through its focus on ecology, creation, poverty, is forming people in a spirituality that is relevant to church and world trends today. Associates are prepared and educated so that they can take their rightful place in the church and the world. Pope John Paul II said of Christian communities (of which associate membership of a religious congregation is an example) that they:

> must be become genuine 'schools' of prayer, where the meeting with Christ is expressed not just in imploring help but also in thanksgiving, praise, adoration contemplation, listening and ardent devotion, until the heart truly 'falls in love'.[9]

Community/Family Spirit/Koinonia

Another of the great needs of people today is to find community, a place where they can grow in love of God and others, a place where they can be themselves and find love, companionship, support and a freedom to express their hopes, fears and struggles. Cardinal Cormac Murphy O'Connor, in his keynote address at the National Conference of Priests in Leeds (2001), said that the future of the church depends on small communities to re-evangelise it.[10] Small communities such as charismatic renewal, the Neo-Catechumenate, Focolare, Christian life communities or associate membership of a religious congregation are all different. The community demands may be loose or quite stringent. But what they have in common is a way of fulfilling that desire on the part of the laity to find community, fellowship, *koinonia*, to find opportunities of sharing prayer and growing in their relationship with God and each other, which can be difficult to find in the large parish church. The church, a sign of community (see Acts 2: 42-27), needs, indeed depends on, religious through their community living and through associate membership to witness to community in a broken world. In a world enslaved by many things – loneliness, a break-down in family life, domestic violence, addictions, unemployment, consumerism, lack of a sense of community and spiritual hunger, associate membership offers a counter witness to what can be achieved when religious and associate members work together to build community, fellowship, *koinonia* based on shared charism, spirituality and mission. Sister Helena O'Donoghue, in an article on the church, stresses that in a world of pain, confusion and instability the 'witness of faithful commitment can only be achieved within a strong sense of community'.[11]

The community aspect of associate membership allows many associates to rediscover the church. It is a source of great hope for the church. It is through people growing together in faith that the church will be renewed. A greater degree of trust and sharing can be built up as the associates grow together in their faith journey. The associates, through their community experience, bring to their parish a deeper prayer, faith and witness to others. They bring new life to the parish. To a very large extent renewal in the church – pastoral, spiritual, and liturgical – will come about through small groups of people being renewed. Associate gatherings are generally characterised by a spirit of welcome, compassion, friendship, openness to each other and readiness and willingness to encourage one another to grow and take seriously their baptismal responsibility to be church. The building of a community of love through associate membership of a religious congregation is a sign and fruit of the love which springs from the heart of the Trinity.[12]

Mission/Ministry/Social Concern

Associate membership is a response to a need within the church today to help the laity take a fuller role in the life and mission of the church. As stressed previously in this book, the Second Vatican Council, in its deep insight into the universal call to holiness and especially in its decree *Apostolicam actuositatem*, helped lay people to rediscover their active role in the church, flowing from their baptism.

By its very nature the Christian vocation is also a vocation to the apostolate. Therefore associate members have become keenly aware of their baptismal calling to mission, and their call to build up the kingdom of God in the world. In this third millennium, an age surely of the laity, the church is more and more aware of the need of evangelisation of people, a task which has been somewhat neglected as the church concentrated on pastoral and catechetical concerns.

The laity are called to a 'new evangelisation' with newness of 'ardour,' 'method' and 'expression'.[13] Associate members come into a heightened awareness of their responsibility for evangelisation as they reflect within their associate groups on what it is to be a disciple of Jesus and their role in the mission of the church. As associate groups grow in love of God and neighbour, they will build up evangelising communities that will be a sign of God's kingdom in the world.

Society needs people who can walk with others in their pain and hopelessness and point them to another way. Associate members are called and challenged to proclaim the kingdom, to share their gifts and talents and support each other in love and trust. At times they can have a practical contribution to make that will ameliorate concrete situations. At other times it will be mainly a presence, being with those in sorrow and need. They are called to a special concern for the poor and marginalised and are challenged to assume a prophetic role in fostering social justice. Associate members are challenged to make a preferential option for the poor, that is for those who 'are-nots' and 'have-nots'. Conscious of the dignity of each person, they strive to create peace and justice for everyone. Seeing all creation as gift, they accept responsibility for the proper use of all things and for care of the earth.[14]

Commitment – An alternative witness
Associate membership offers an alternative witness to the world. Today the world desperately needs people of vision, people who will speak a word of light and hope. Associate members are committed to being instruments of love and healing to whomsoever the Lord puts in their paths, especially the poor and marginalised. The word of God, which they commit themselves to reflect on in their prayer time, challenges them to be people who work for peace and justice in society and in the world. The associate's commitment or response is a light in

darkness; it contradicts greed and the abuse of power in a selfish world. It is a witness to walking in the footsteps of Jesus, to taking up the cross everyday and following him who is the way, the truth and the light.

Their commitment or response is always in an attitude of openness and humility in the deep realisation of the dignity of all people and that they too are in a position of receiving from them. It is in the realisation of their own weakness and need of the love and mercy of God that they can make a commitment/ response.

Formation
Christian formation will be more effective when it takes place in the context of community. An associate formation programme offers the associates opportunities to develop a spirituality suitable for their lives as lay people in the world. They become aware of their call to holiness in the everyday circumstances of their life. As they become increasingly aware of the secular role of the laity they see the importance of their work in economics, culture, technology and in all areas of society. Spirituality is not like a table of buffet dishes all ready for consumption. It is a search, a journey in which each person is different and must find his or her way with the help of a heritage. Unless the notion of search or journey is emphasised, formation will become formal or static.

The associates are led in the understanding that the call to mission is not a privilege of religious or the clergy but that it is a challenge to every person who has been baptisied. The task and challenge of formation for mission is being met within the associate formation programme where the associates are also being educated and formed in current church teachings and theological trends.

Pope John Paul II spoke of the need to examine how the documents of Vatican II and the subsequent church documents have been received. He stated how 'the council documents have lost nothing of their value or brilliance' with the passing of the years.[15] He went on to state that they need to be read correctly, to be widely known and taken to heart as important and normative texts. Associate membership offers opportunities for this to happen. There are many members of religious communities and associates capable of doing this in a competent manner. Some associate groups already have a formation programme or now realise the need for one. These programmes allow for ongoing growth and renewal. Some of these groups have an associate manual or handbook where there is input on a wide variety of topics, questions for reflection, appropriate numbers from constitutions, sayings of the founder, passages of scripture and church documents. These can provide a rich source for reflection and prayer.

Strengths and Weaknesses of Associate Membership

Evaluation is important for all endeavours, whether new or well established. Without evaluation an initial vision can become blurred, elements can be missed, deviations or negative features can imperceptibly arise. However, it is important that evaluation be realistic and appropriate for the stage of an endeavour. In the case of associate membership any evaluation must necessarily be interim. It is nevertheless worth doing. The fact that associates appreciate their membership and that groups of associates are growing is itself positive, if subjective evidence. A more objective evaluation can be made by comparing associate membership against the aims expressed at the World Congress of Ecclesial Movements and New Communities (1999). These aims were:

- to celebrate unity in diversity (1 Cor 12: 4).
- to give thanks for all that God has brought about in individual lives in the church and in the world through the movements and new communities.
- to recognise the fidelity of the ecclesial movements and new communities to the gifts they have received, to a deeper ecclesial self-awareness, and to a more generous participation in the life and mission of their local churches.
- to commit themselves to a greater missionary responsibility for those to whom the gospel has not yet been proclaimed.
- to commit themselves to a more fruitful spirit of charity in responding to the needs of humankind and in developing more acceptable lifestyles for everyone.

It is obvious from the previous chapters that associate membership of religious congregations is largely fulfilling these aims. Associate members can truly rejoice in diversity. They share in the charism of their particular congregation, bringing to it another emphasis and style of living. They share in a spirituality but live it according to their particular lifestyle and in a way that is relevant to their lay state. The religious and associates come together for various activities, both social and spiritual, where each celebrates his/her own uniqueness. The way they live out their mission again will differ but they will support and collaborate with each other in living it out. It is at the centre of the church that they live out their mission. This is of key importance, that the church benefits from the formation, charism and spirituality of associates and opens them to greater missionary responsibility and to the needs of the world, especially those who are marginalised in any way.

Associate membership offers to associates four characteristics which are essential to church:

- *Kerygma* (the Word)
- *Leitourgia* (Worship)
- *Koinonia* (Community)
- *Diakonia* (Ministry or Service)

These four characteristics, which were present in the early church, are important if the church is to be vibrant and alive. The word about God's love, about the kingdom and the Lordship of Jesus needs to be proclaimed so that people can be evangelised. This leads to worship, builds community so that people can go out in mission and service to proclaim and witness to God's kingdom on earth. Associate membership allows the associates to experience this. The Word is proclaimed, *kergma*, leading to worship, *leitourgia*, community, *koinonia* is built up and the associates go out in mission and service, *diakonia*.

Associates are supported and encouraged to be at the centre of the church and its mission by having:

- A common Mission
- Shared values and beliefs
- Clear goals
- A climate conducive to developing charism, spirituality, community, mission and commitment
- A formation programme
- Religious and lay involvement

If we were further to consider the lists of fruits of association given in the apostolic exhortation *Christifideles laici* which should be evident in a group of associate members of a religious congregation, we will see that many of these fruits are present and that there is a strong sense of commitment.[16]

- Among associate members there is a renewed appreciation of prayer, contemplation and sacramental life.
- Many associates have been given a new understanding of their marriage and a new understanding of priestly and religious life.
- There is among associates a readiness to participate in programmes and church activities at local, national and international level.
- There is a commitment among them to be Christian witnesses in the various situations of social life.
- Associates have a strong commitment to catechesis and Christian formation.
- They have a spirit of detachment and evangelical poverty leading to greater sharing with the poor.
- Being an associate member has led to conversion and a return to the church and sacraments of some who had fallen away.

In this chapter we have, as it were, taken a still snap-shot of associate membership of a religious congregation. It is a rapidly evolving phenomenon in the church today. We are privileged to see lay spirituality emerge under our very eyes. What we have seen can give a sure discernment that here is a work of the Holy Spirit. Whilst the main lines are clear, the Spirit is drawing religious and laity in partnership into a future known only to God.

The Way Ahead

In this chapter there has been a very positive evaluation of the potential of associate membership. The way ahead can easily be stated as a hope that associate membership will expand and develop. There are, however, areas of possible weakness and tension.

The Religious Institutes

Even in those institutes which have associate membership not all religious are necessarily enthusiastic. Some religious need to recognise the importance of this new development in the church. Other tired religious cannot see themselves with energy to encourage this new form. Again we find religious who are distrustful of the whole notion of associate membership. There are those who find it hard to allow lay leadership to emerge. There is a further problem when individual religious are disillusioned in their own commitment. Perhaps the most serious problem among religious is to regard associate membership as a form of piety rather than a spirituality. Hence the importance of the notions we have treated at length such as charism, mission, community, commitment. One would hope that positive experiences of lay associate membership will help to dispel doubts, apathy or anxiety concerning a new expression of their religious heritage.

The Associates

The lay associate members can easily hinder or slow down the development of this new form of life. Throughout this work we have continually stressed the notion of lay spirituality, but we find lay people who are so conscious of their lay identity that they fear contamination from the culture of religious life. They can be excessively suspicious of structures. They have to realise that the heritage they are offered was originally packaged in a religious institute and that there is a serious challenge in leaving the wrapping aside and concentrating on the gift. A further problem arises from counter cultural values prized in religious life, like asceticism or self denial. There is a temptation for lay people to approach the spirituality of religious life as if it were *à la carte*, whereas the secret of the religious institute is precisely its integration of many elements in a unified whole. A final difficulty can arise when men seek to be associate members in a feminine institute (often in company with their wives) The charism has been incarnated in a feminine form and men have to discern how it may be lived by them as males. A similar pattern can be experienced by women associates in a male congregation but to a lesser degree, perhaps. Women have long been exposed to the Christian message coming to them in masculine language and symbols.

Religious and lay associate members are journeying together to accept a new work of the Holy Spirit. Neither group can know the form in which lay associate membership will emerge. There is necessarily a difficult dialogue in which religious and laity must respect the charism of the other. Neither group can see itself as the one with greater wisdom. A desire to be taught by laity must mark the approach of religious; a desire to learn from religious must be the mark of lay people. Both religious and lay need a profound desire to be taught by the Holy Spirit who is once more doing a new thing in the church.

From the day of Pentecost the Holy Spirit, 'sent continually to sanctify the church' (*LG* 4), has not ceased to do new things to build up the holy Catholic Church.

In the early Church he sustained ministers and preachers in their proclamation of the good news; the church thus spread very rapidly in the Mediterranean Basin. Soon there were persecutions and the Spirit gave strength to martyrs to witness to Jesus by suffering and death; the blood of martyrs was the seed of the church. After the time of martyrs, the Spirit inspired hermits and monks to preach by their lives that wealth and secular power were not absolute values; people recognised these callings as profoundly attractive. In the Middle Ages the Spirit inspired charismatic figures like Dominic and Francis to found the friar movement. After the Reformation the Spirit led people to found active religious congregations to look after social, mental and educational needs; huge numbers joined these new-styled forms of religious life. With Vatican II the call to lay holiness, always present in the church, began to germinate and produce new fruits. After the council we find new strong lay movements. The religious families now saw a way of sharing and enriching their heritage through lay associate membership of their congregations.

We seem to be in relatively early days of this new work of the Spirit. With new communities one might expect this work to expand rapidly. Church leaders, such as popes, bishops and superiors of religious congregations have looked at this phenomen and judged it authentic. We can now look with confidence at this new work and leave the unknown to the Spirit who draws us into a future known by God. The challenge for us is to seize this moment, of grace, this new opportunity for religious and their associates. Associate membership is new. The biblical process has been done.

> Do not suppress the Spirit; test everything, hold on to what is good. (1 Thess 5:19-21)
>
> We must gather all that the Lord gives us lest anything should be wasted. (see Jn 6:12)

FURTHER READING

John Paul II, Apostolic Exhortation, *Tertio millennio adveniente* (1994)
John Paul II, Apostolic Letter, *Novo millennio ineunte*, (2001)

NOTES

1. See John Paul II, Apostolic Letter, *Novo millennio ineunte*, (2001) no 32
2. Ibid
3. Ibid 43
4. D. J. O'Leary, *New Hearts, New Models: A Spirituality for Priests*, (Dublin: Columba Press, 1997)
5. See John Paul II, Apostolic Letter, *Novo millennio ineunte*, nos 31-32
6. Ibid 31
7. Ibid 34
8. See S.D. Sammon, 'Is Religious Life Dying?' *Human Development* 19 (1998) 5-14 at 14.
9. *Novo millennio ineunte*, no 33
10. See C. Murphy-O'Connor , 'A Song on 'Alien Soil'', *The Tablet* (15 September 2001) 1314-1316
11. See H. O'Donoghue, Is the Irish Church in Crisis?' *The Furrow* 44 (1993) 67-77 at 75-76.
12. Ibid 43
13. See John Paul II, Apostolic Exhortation, *Tertio millennio adveniente* (1994)
14. See *The Catechism of the Catholic Church* 293-325; 2415-2418; see also *Novo millennio ineunte* 50-51.
15. See *Novo millennio ineunte* 57
16. See *CL* 30